DIVIDE and CONQUER
Book 2

BY **François Lemaire de Ruffieu**

XENOPHON PRESS

Published by Xenophon Press LLC

7518 Bayside Road, Franktown, Virginia 23354-2106, U.S.A.

ISBN-10:0933316941
ISBN-13:9780933316942
Cover painting by François Lemaire de Ruffieu.

DIVIDE and CONQUER
Book 2

BY François Lemaire de Ruffieu

*These pages are dedicated to all my students
and riders I have yet to meet.*

AVANT PROPOS

*D*ivide and Conquer Book II is a further study of *Divide and Conquer Book I*, in which I explain how to develop the Low School and High School dressage movements. To obtain the best results, it is important to have read and studied the materials proposed in Book I.

Doctrine

The expression of a doctrine or style is a reflection of the tradition of a nation, its culture and horse breeding. The French culture, steeped in its long history of Latin influence, is seen in the people's fondness of liberty and a tendency towards less rigid disciplines. French horses have been bred for brilliance, temperament, and delicacy. The French doctrine rejects all work by use of force and advocates equitation through developing strength and flexibility.

Equitation is the art of developing the horse's muscular system to enhance the springiness of movement. To manage the horse's power, one must be able to blend impulsion with flexibility. These two elements, however, cannot be combined in the same manner. For sport horses, racing, combined training and jumping, greater emphasis is placed on impulsion versus flexibility of the horse's muscular system. For the dressage horse, the rapport must be equal.

In French Equitation, training focuses on flexibility:

Direct Flexion *(Ramener)* is the flexibility of the poll area (atlas-axis).

Collection *(Rassembler)* is the flexibility of the loins area

Lightness *(Légèreté)*, at its supreme degree, is elastic flexibility, a quality of instantaneous obedience to the rider's aids.

Before the horse's muscular system can flex and stretch, there must be motion with impulsion.

Impulsion is obedience to the rider's legs and the ability to maintain the activity of the horse's posterior limbs.

Flexibility can only be achieved by discipline and by molding the entire muscular system. By combining longitudinal and lateral exercises, impulsion is generated with cadence by means of gentle and steady alternation of muscular contraction and relaxation.

Figure 1 - The Rider

TABLE OF CONTENTS

LIST OF ILLUSTRATIONS

PREFACE

Dressage is an Art, and as in any art, it can be viewed in many different ways. History shows that some extraordinary Riding Masters had radically different training theories. Different schools of thought, riders' physiques, and differences in horse breeds have influenced riding masters, leaving us a rich history of teachings with which to properly educate our horses.

Dressage tends to follow fashion. Nevertheless, the goals of dressage have always remained the same: render the horse agreeable, easy to ride, well-balanced, and yielding to the rider's slightest aids. Dressage is a school of obedience and a school of thought.

Although many wonderful methods have been written, the study that I provide in these books has worked well for my students and has the benefit of remaining true to Classical, *i.e.,* natural methods.

Horses are not born knowing dressage movements. Riders must learn the movements first, prior to training their horses. Daily practice allows for subtle repetition. During the progression of schooling in dressage, riders and trainers should always remember the wisdom of General L'Hotte (1825 - 1904):

Calm, Forward and Straight

Calm: The horse's mind should be completely at peace; disorder generates imponderables. Calm is the essential element of submission and necessary for the progression of dressage.

Forward: The horse must be obedient to the rider's slightest leg action and must always be willing to move forward. Lack of a horse's willingness to respond promptly to the rider's aids renders him useless.

Straight: The horse's attributes and body parts must move in harmony and be properly aligned. The absence of this harmony results in disunited locomotion, crookedness, and improper balance.

The rider must train the horse from back to front. When the rider emphasizes training from the front end, the neck muscles compress and hinder the muscular development of the horse's top line. As a result, the horse's natural locomotion deteriorates and the body is harmed. The horse's gaits must remain natural to induce the horse to use his top line muscles.

It is important to remember that horses are not naturally symmetrical. When they are in motion, horses have a tendency to traverse themselves. For the proper evolution of their dressage, it is most important for horses to be straight and symmetrical. Training should encourage the horse to maintain his bipeds [lateral pairs of legs] equidistant and parallel when working on a straight line or on a circle of any diameter.

On a straight line, the horse's spine should remain straight and the activity of each posterior should be equal; the thrust is transmitted from back to front.

On a curved path of travel, the horse's spine marries the shape of the circle with ease; the horse bears equal weight on both sides. The outside biped is further away from the center of the radius and the inside biped is closer to the center of the arc or circle. The outside posterior pushes more than it engages, and the inside posterior engages more than it pushes. We can easily understand that work on a circle allows the development of the amplification of the walk and the trot by virtue of the extension of the external biped and the flexion of the internal biped. The first stage of generating straightness is a frank locomotion toward the demanded destination without any torsion or contraction. From the beginning, riding should be *calm, forward, and straight.*

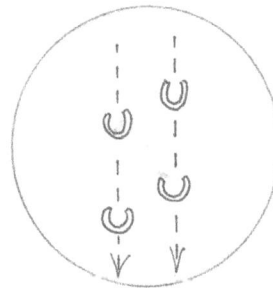

lateral bipeds parallel
on a straight line

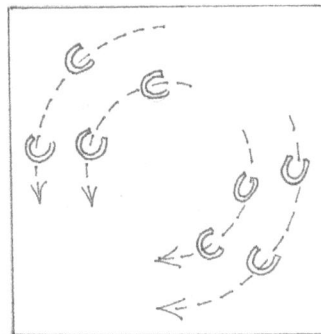

lateral bipeds parallel on a circle

Figure 2 – Horse moving straight

How can the rider determine the asymmetry of the horse?

To determine the natural symmetry of the horse's locomotion, the rider should employ a simple test as follows: Riding the horse on loose reins, traveling to the right on the long side of the arena, heading away from the stable, the rider should restrain herself from making any corrections except to observe how well the horse remains on track. The rider should repeat this test by traveling on the opposite long side of the arena, again, thus by heading away from the stable.

When the horse is not symmetrical, the rider will be aware that the horse will veer more or less toward the center of the arena. If the horse veers toward the left it means that the horse's left posterior engages more than the right while propelling less than the right (it will be the opposite if the horse veers to the right). Consequently, the horse's right posterior will engage less and propel more. This lack of equality incites the horse to veer toward the left. The rider would feel that the horse is resisting against her left leg and is seeking more contact with the right rein. The horse's avoidance of connection with the left rein causes asymmetrical contact with the rider's hands. As a result, when circling left, the horse will have the tendency to widen the curve and bend his neck to the left. When circling right, the horse will shorten his turn on the right shoulder, i.e. drop his right shoulder, while his head continues to the left.

To better exploit the horse's natural propulsion of the posteriors, the rider should maintain straightness in the horse's entire body so that he will propel himself equally with both posteriors towards his anterior. When the shoulders and the haunches are aligned and straight, the horse will be balanced. The rider should always seek equal contact on the reins by lengthening the rein that feels short as opposed to shortening the rein that feels long. The rider's hands must always be gentle, respecting the horse's mouth.

While practicing all lateral exercises, since the horse's shoulders, in this example, have the tendency to veer to the left while the haunches move to the right, the horse's asymmetry will be less noticeable. By becoming aware of this inequality, the rider should learn which exercises will help correct the asymmetry and teach the horse to equally engage both posteriors to develop their thrusting power and render suppleness to the shoulders.

In Equitation, "To feel is to understand."

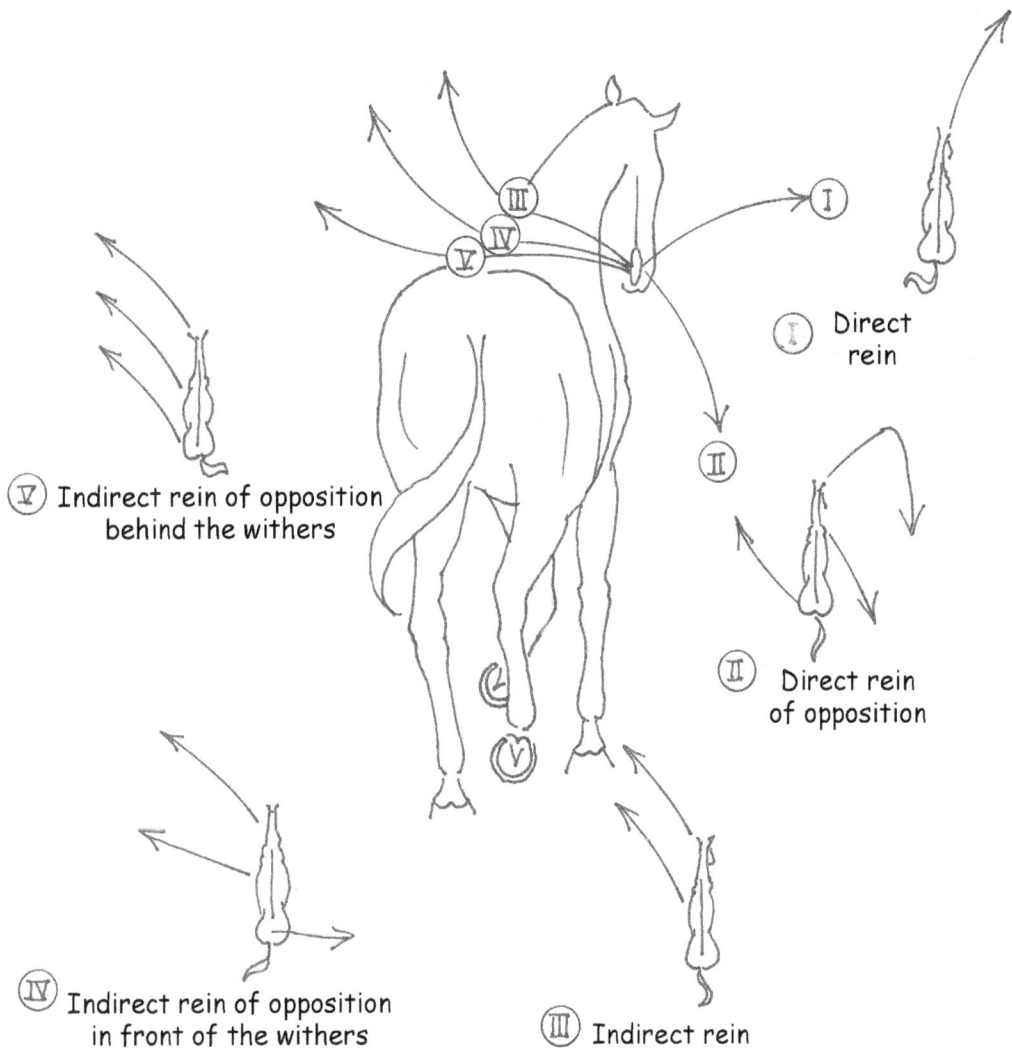

Figure 3 - Five Rein Effects

There are five rein effects:

1. The *direct rein*, also known as the *leading rein*
2. The *direct rein of opposition*
3. The *indirect rein*, also known as the *neck rein*
4. The *indirect rein of opposition in front of the withers*
5. The *indirect rein of opposition behind the withers*

INTRODUCTION

As the horse's training evolves, riders and trainers will encounter various situations requiring decisions. Problems cause one to think, to analyze, to create, and to progress. In studying the work of the Masters, the mind is broadened. One quickly realizes that one should not be afraid of making a wrong choice. One may also realize that there are many choices that are neither right nor wrong. Instead, one choice might produce a more preferred result. As long as the horse is treated properly in his education, the outcome of right or wrong, good or bad is rarely measurable.

One might consider the wisdom of an ancient Zen tale:

> *A farmer, who had recently acquired a stallion, ran to the local Zen Master in much distress, calling, "Master, Master, my horse, my only horse is gone. My stallion has run away, and I cannot plow my fields."*
>
> *The Zen Master peacefully replied, "Who knows if it is good or bad that he ran away?"*
>
> *Feeling most disheartened, the farmer returns home, but two days later, he returns to the Zen Master overjoyed, "Master, Master, my stallion is back. He returned and brought two mares."*
>
> *The Zen Master replied, "Who knows if it is good or bad?"*
>
> *Three days later the farmer returns and tearfully explains that his only son and helper has broken his leg while trying to ride one of the mares. His son, with his leg in a cast, cannot work.*
>
> *The Zen Master replied, "Who knows if it is good or bad?"*
>
> *A few days later the King's soldiers came to the farm to conscript young men to fight in war. The farmer's son, still incapacitated, was passed over. "Who knows if it is good or bad?"*

As one can see, the story never ends. One never knows whether the choices are good or bad under the circumstances or the ramifications of one's choices. Riding Masters of the past have left us a vast myriad reservoir of ideas. In the military, we recollect the teachings of our predecessors and study their work.

CHAPTER ONE

For the horse to be pleasant and easy to ride, both sides of the horse's body need to be equally supple. Riders should alternate longitudinal and lateral exercises to unlock adductor and abductor muscles to allow more freedom to both extensor and flexor muscles. The horse's entire muscular system should be invited to work to develop suppleness and strength as well as to develop cardiovascular fitness.

In progressing through dressage, the walk is said to be the learning gait and the trot is said to be the working gait. The canter is the result of the work in the walk and the trot or the "proof of nine,"[1] so to speak.

The walk is fundamental to learning; the trot is fundamental of agility and one of the first skills imparted to the horse. Walking and trotting on a straight line or on a circle provides the horse with power in his forward motion through his limbs, shoulders and haunches, but it does not develop the horse's agility and aptitude to cross one leg over the other. Combining longitudinal and lateral exercises enables the horse to develop power and agility.

The horse's true balance translates to ease in the longitudinal and lateral movements and perfect access to the entire muscular system.

Longitudinal Exercises

Longitudinal exercises favor the flexibility of the horse's top line and therefore induce the engagement of the hindquarters and the mobility of the haunches by developing the flexibility of the sacroiliac and coxo-femoral joints. Opening and closing these joints allows the horse to bring his hocks under his body. Springlike, the horse must be able to stretch and compress his muscles to allow elasticity.

While longitudinal exercises have the advantage of developing power of the posteriors by stretching and compressing the extensor and flexor muscles that are used for engagement, impulsion and straightness, they tend to cause hollowing and stiffening of the horse's spinal column. Longitudinal exercises also have the

---

1   A simple, rapid method to check multiplication or division, as widely used by the French speaking people, almost entirely unknown in the United States. — *Editor's Note*

disadvantage of causing the horse to develop resistances if they are practiced for too long a period or if performed at a rapid pace. If they are performed at too slow a pace, the horse will create defenses. For best results, the transitions should be practiced very frequently but, for brief periods of time. The rider should discover a comfortable pace for each individual horse.

Longitudinal exercises generally include transitions from one gait to another and alternating the speed within each gait. The transitions range from the simplest, walk—halt—walk, to the most difficult, canter—rein-back—canter. The transitions can be demanded while the horse is traveling on a straight line, on a circle, or while progressing laterally on three or four tracks. The purpose of longitudinal exercises is to enable the horse to go from a collected state to a state of total extension and vice versa.

When the horse is collected, the horse lowers his haunches. The collection is demonstrated in correct Piaffe and when performing a canter pirouette. Collection is the flexion of the horse's loins that incite the horse to bend at the hocks and to engage his posteriors under his body toward his center of gravity. Stated simply, the horse shortens his base of support (also called the "polygon of sustentation"), i.e. the space between the horse's anterior and posterior feet.

Alternating speed and changing gaits every few strides are important exercises for both the horse and rider. In a downward transition the horse should gain in height what he loses in length. In an upward transition, the horse will gain in length what he loses in height. In this manner, the horse's body can be thought of as a spring in which the body stretches and compresses at the rider's demand. The ability of the horse and rider to accomplish these transitions is necessary preparation for all future exercises.

Benefits for the Horse

The transitions render the horse attentive to the rider's legs and hands and provoke the engagement of the posteriors by shortening the gait in downward transitions. The posteriors are unlocked by lengthening the gaits. When the transitions are performed in close intervals, the horse will remain alert.

Benefits for the Rider

Transitions enable the rider to create, maintain, and regulate impulsion. They also enable the rider to properly coordinate the legs and hands while applying these actions separately. The rider's legs create energy in the horse's hindquarters (propulsive aids) while the rider's hands monitor this energy (regulating aids). The rider's legs and hands should never act simultaneously but should act separately. Applying Master François Baucher's motto will become fundamental:

"Legs without hands and hands without legs."

The following longitudinal exercises should be repeated daily 5 to 10 times in each direction. If the horse is obedient and performs well, 5 or 6 times should be sufficient. No more than ten repetitions should be requested in a daily session. Excess repetition in anything is rarely a good thing.

Exercises at the Walk

Study at the Walk

1. Walk — Halt — Walk
2. Lengthen — Shorten — Lengthen
3. Lengthen — Halt — Lengthen
4. Walk — Halt — Rein-back — Walk
5. Walk — rein-back — Walk

Nota Bene

Because the horse's mouth is very sensitive, the rider should never pull on the reins to halt the horse. Pulling incites the horse to pull against the rider.

If the horse does not respond quickly to the demand of a downward transition, the rider should proceed as follows:

1. Resist with both legs in steady contact.

2. Supinate both hands. Rotate the hands so that the wrist and palm face upward with the thumbs to the outside.

3. Slowly elevate both hands in a vertical plane until the horse slows and comes to a complete halt.

4. As soon as the horse halts, the rider should lower the hands, soften the legs and hands as well as release contact with the horse's mouth. This is known as the descent of the hands.

If the horse does not stop, the likely cause is poor balance. Since the horse is on his forehand, the rider, by elevating the hands, lifts the base of the horse's neck and allows the horse to transfer his weight from his forehand towards the hindquarters. The horse regains his balance. With time and practice, the horse will learn to promptly reorganize himself and regain balance without necessitating the rider to elevate the hands. Elevating the hands is a wonderful tool for the rider because it eliminates any necessity to pull on the horse's mouth and causes no pain for the horse, if used with tact.

Exercises at the Trot

The trot is an essential gait for the dressage because the horse's legs will be displaced symmetrically while neck oscillations are minimized. The trot contributes to the development of the muscular system and to proper cardiac and pulmonary function.

Study at the Trot

1. Trot — Walk — Trot
2. Trot — Walk — Halt — Walk — Trot

As the horse improves his performance, the rider should gradually reduce the number of walk steps until, one day, the horse is able to:

3. Trot — Halt — Trot

4. Gradually lengthen and shorten the trot strides. As the horse responds more promptly, the rider should increase and decrease the speed in each session until, one day, the horse, from a very energetic pace, will be nearly able to trot in one spot.

5. Trot — Walk — Halt — Rein-back — Walk — Trot
6. Trot — Walk — Rein-back — Walk — Trot
7. Trot — Rein-back — Trot.

Exercises at the Canter

Study at the Canter

1. Canter — Trot — Canter
2. Canter — Trot — Walk — Trot — Canter

As the horse improves performing these transitions, the rider should gradually reduce the number of trotting strides until, one day, the horse is able to progress to Number 3.

3. Canter — Walk — Halt — Walk — Canter

Following the same progression, the rider should gradually reduce the walking steps until the horse is able to progress to Numbers 4 through 7.

4. Canter — Halt — Canter

5. Canter — Halt — Rein-back — Canter

6. Canter — Walk — Rein-back — Canter

7. Canter — Rein-back — Canter

Chronophotography shows that when a horse performs a canter departure from the trot, the horse has the tendency to propel himself from his anteriors. When the canter departure is demanded from the walk, halt, or rein-back, however, the horse propels his body primarily from the posteriors.

As soon as the horse is ready, the rider should work with the horse to perfect the transitions walk—canter—walk; halt—canter—halt, and rein-back—canter—rein-back. This study will be invaluable when beginning to practice the flying changes of lead.

Gradually, the horse's obedience should manifest instantaneously. Every time the horse has a tendency to resist the rider's hands to slow the pace, the rider should restudy all the transitions at the walk. As the horse becomes more obedient and capable of easily switching from one speed to another, the lengthening and shortenings should be demanded more frequently and at closer intervals. This work-study consists of balancing the horse's body between the rider's legs and hands. The rider must always insist on the horse's prompt obedience.

With a cold or lethargic horse, the lengthenings and upward transitions should be demanded with greater insistence. With an electric or over-active horse, shortening the length of strides and downward transitions should be demanded with greater insistence.

When this work-study is well-understood by the horse, the rider should demand the same exercises following the pattern of circles, serpentines, half-voltes, etc. At first, these turns should have a wide diameter. As the horse gradually performs these curved patterns with greater ease, the radius can be gradually reduced to obtain more engagement from the inside posterior and further suppleness of the horse's spinal column.

Modern dressage competitions have codified various types of trot that are related to the horse's body position:

Working Trot

The working trot is the pace between the collected trot and the medium trot. This trot is used when the horse has not yet progressed in his training to accomplish the collected movements. At the working trot the horse shows proper balance and remains on the bit, goes forward with even, elastic steps, and good hock action, which underlines the importance of impulsion originating from the hindquarters.

Trot Lengthening or Lengthening of Stride

The trot lengthening is a variation between the working and medium trot in which a horse has not yet progressed to sustaining the medium trot.

Collected Trot

The horse remains on the bit, moves forward with the neck raised and arched. The hocks, being well-engaged and flexed, must maintain energetic impulsion enabling the shoulders to move with greater mobility, thereby demonstrating complete self-carriage. Although the horse's steps are shorter than at the other trots, the horse maintains elasticity and cadence.

Medium Trot

This is a pace of moderate lengthening compared to the extended trot, and the horse appears more rounded than he does when performing the extended trot. The horse moves forward with lengthened steps, without hurrying, and with impulsion from the hindquarters. The rider allows the horse to lower his head and neck slightly and to carry his head somewhat in front of the vertical. The steps should be even. The entire movement is balanced and unconstrained.

Extended Trot

At the extended trot, the horse covers as much ground as possible. Without rushing, the steps are lengthened to the utmost. This results from great impulsion from the hind quarters. The rider allows the horse to lengthen the frame and to gain ground while controlling the poll. The forefeet should touch the ground on the spot towards which they point when fully extended. The anterior and posterior legs should reach equally forward in the moment of extension. The entire movement should be well-balanced, and the transition to the collected trot should be smoothly executed by putting greater weight on the hindquarters.

Speed is not a criterion of impulsion.

Exercises to Lengthen the Trot

1. Practice prompt transitions from a forward canter to a forward trot, and back to a forward canter. Repeat many times, progressively faster and at closer intervals.

2. Following the pattern of a large circle, the horse should be maintained in a counter shoulder-in (shoulder-out) to better engage the outside posterior, and to develop the agility of the outside anterior. After one or two revolutions, the rider should leave the circle and send the horse vigorously forward following the pattern of a straight line in either direction.

Figure 4 - Counter Shoulder-in on a circle

Nota Bene

When the horse performs the lengthening well and truly opens his strides, the rider should have the feeling that the horse is moving slower rather than faster.

After opening the trot (and also when working at the canter), it would be wise for the rider to bring the horse back to a full halt and drop the reins to encourage the horse to rebalance himself and to regain calmness. This practice will help the rider easily collect the horse after the extension.

Exercises to Shorten the Trot

1. The rider should practice and perfect obtaining brisk but smooth downward and upward transitions from trot to walk and from walk to trot.

2. The rider should practice the transitions trot—walk—halt—walk—trot and then gradually eliminate the walk steps in order to obtain trot—halt—trot.

3. The rider should gradually reduce the speed of the trot without sacrificing the activity of the hindquarters. The rider's hands should be acting by opening and closing the fingers on the reins while the legs are resisting.

A horse may seem to be progressing slowly at performing proper lengthening or shortening of the gaits because, at the beginning, the horse does not engage his haunches enough and his top line is still stiff. When excessive lengthening or shortening is demanded too soon, the horse will hollow and stiffen his top line or will resist by lifting or lowering his neck and head. It would be better to wait until the horse is mentally and physically ready to perform these exercises so that he willingly gives the rider what is being demanded of him.

CHAPTER TWO

Lateral Exercises

Traveling sideways is not natural to the horse. Although horses at liberty sometimes move laterally to run away from something that is frightening to them, horses are herbivores and will innately run forward to avoid danger.

Lateral exercises are studied and practiced for the benefit of the horse's education and physical development. Riders also benefit from practice coordinating their natural aids laterally and diagonally. Traveling sideways helps ameliorate the horse's awkwardness, while heightening his aptitude for preserving and modifying his equilibrium, enhancing his agility and helping him regain the natural freedom of his locomotion.

Lateral exercises are said to be done on three or four tracks. When the horse travels sideways, his forehand and hindquarters follow different tracks. The goals of these exercises are to amplify the general mobility and flexibility of the horse, develop agility of the forehand, allow for engagement of the hindquarters, and generate greater flexibility in his loins and improve articulation in all limbs.

The effort of crossing over conjoining limbs can only be entirely exploited at the walk and trot. At the canter, the horse has the tendency to leap to avoid crossing of the legs.

While lateral exercises have the advantage of developing suppleness of the spinal column, they have the inconvenience of retarding the impulsion.

In lateral movements, the horse must remain calm so that the movements do not cause harm. If the horse is not at peace, the muscles can contract, defeating the purpose of the exercises. When traveling laterally, the horse must maintain the same pace (without slowing). The rider should always be mindful and maintain the horse's tempo and activity by closing both legs intermittently instead of on every stride.

Nota Bene

By alternating between longitudinal and lateral movements, a complementary effect of the exercises is generated. The shortcomings of one are offset by the benefits of the other. This synergy of combining exercises is essential in the horse's training. The rider should always emphasize the forward movement in the lateral exercises over the sideways or crossing movement.

The angles of the lateral work determine the engagement and the crossing of the hind legs. When traveling on three parallel tracks, the horse will emphasize the engagement of the inside posterior. When traveling on four tracks, the horse crosses his inside posterior to a greater degree than for engagement. Recall that in Divide and Conquer Book 1, the horse was said to be engaging when he brought his hind legs under his body toward his center of gravity.

Two Simple Exercises to Initiate the Horse to Lateral Work

Exercise One: On a Circle

Start at the walk on a small circle (approximately 10 meters in diameter) tracking right. The horse's spine will be bent from back to front. The rider should laterally and tangentially move away from the circle by simultaneously applying a right indirect rein of opposition in front of the withers to displace the horse's shoulders while maintaining the right leg at the girth (yielding to the legs).

After several sideways steps, the rider should guide the horse to travel forward and straight to prevent any resistance because the horse is not yet fit to travel laterally for too long a period. Daily repetition of this simple exercise and a gradual increase in the number of sideways steps develops the lateral mobility and prevents resistance. The rider should repeat this exercise tracking in the opposite direction, as all exercises should be mirrored.

Figure 5 - Three and four tracks

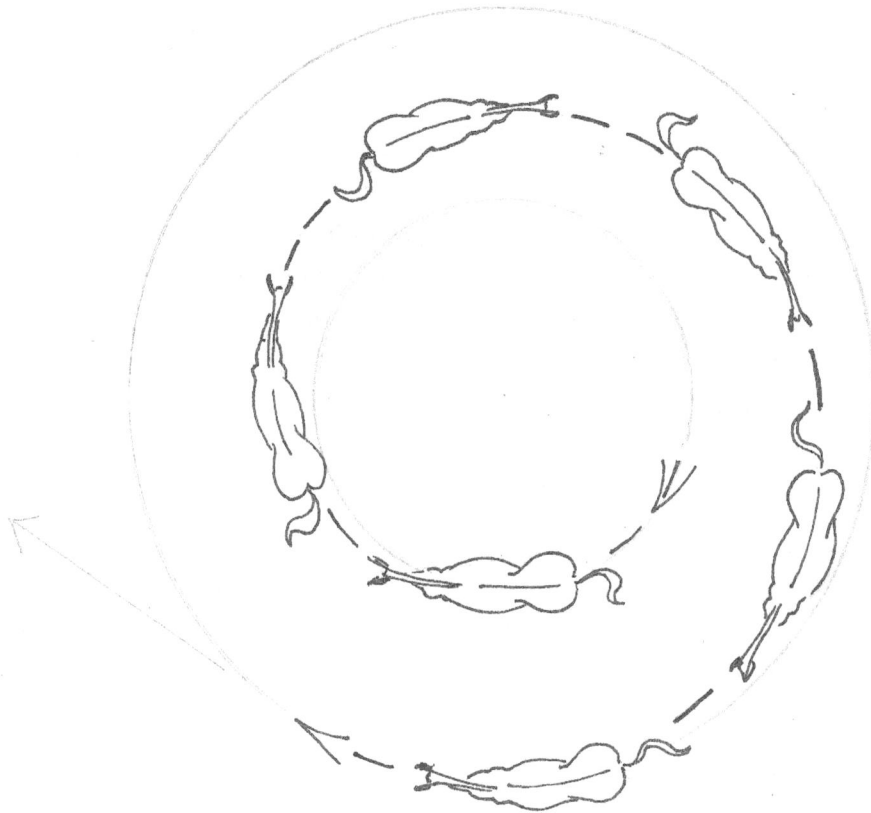

Figure 6 - Small circle drifting to a large circle

Exercise Two. On a Straight Line

Beginning at the walk, tracking left, the rider should follow the long side of the arena on an inside track (about 4-6 feet from the wall or enclosure) and gradually leave this inside track by leading the horse to the right toward the wall using a right direct rein. By maintaining a concave (to the right) body position, the horse should follow the enclosure of the arena and maintain an angle of 30° to 35° to the wall. The rider does this by applying a right indirect rein behind the withers with the right leg at the girth to maintain the horse's bend to the right. After a few sideways steps, the rider should straighten the horse's body by applying a right indirect rein by moving the right hand slightly more forward and to the left so as to displace the horse's shoulders in front of his haunches and then stimulate the pace to activate the hind legs. Gradually, over a period of several training sessions, the rider should increase the number of lateral steps to better condition the horse's body. The horse becomes more comfortable while traveling in this sideways position. Repeating the same exercise in the other direction develops symmetry.

Traveling while facing the wall is an interesting pedagogic method that can be used to teach the horse to move sideways correctly. While it requires little effort by the rider to guide the horse, the horse has an inconvenient tendency to reduce the activity of his hindquarters due to his fear of feeling confined. Sometimes, in training, one must be prepared to sacrifice something for the benefit of another. The wall should be used only for a few sessions or while the horse is still in the learning phase of the exercise.

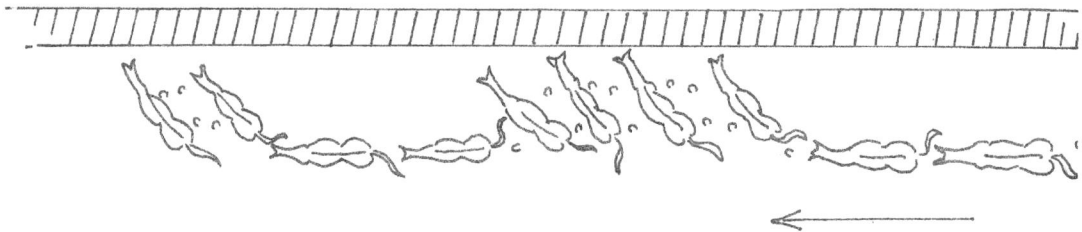

Figure 7 - Lateral work facing a wall.

Nota Bene:

An even spinal bend is necessary for performing all lateral exercises.

The horse's bend is the consequence of the costal (ribcage) flexion obtained by the rider's leg acting at the girth, supported by outside leg behind the girth and the rider's inside hand to maintain the horse's bend, known as the corridor of the aids. To obtain and maintain the horse's bend, the rider should:

1. Position the outside leg back to incite the horse to displace his haunches toward the rider's receiving inside leg at the girth to maintain the bend.

2. The rider should maintain the position of horse's nose to the inside with the inside hand while using the outside hand to release and allow the action of the inside hand. The inside hand can then regulate the action, as necessary.

3. The rider should first distribute his/her weight equally between the two seat bones and then shift his/her weight toward the direction of the motion, i.e. weight on the outside stirrup.

Figure 8 - Corridor of the aids

The two most important lateral exercises are the Shoulder-In and the Half-Pass. All other exercises are merely a means to an end.

Shoulder-In

The shoulder-in has its heritage in the eighteenth century. The venerable François Robichon de La Guérinière (1688 - 1751), First Ecuyer at the Riding Academy of Paris, has been attributed the paternity of the shoulder-in exercise by adapting ideas expounded from Monsieur Salomon de La Broue and William Cavendish, Duke of Newcastle.

Monsieur de La Guérinière explained that the shoulder-in exercise has many benefits that "I regard as the alpha and omega of all exercises for a horse that are intended to develop complete suppleness and perfect agility of all parts. The shoulder-in is the first and the last lesson that you give to your horse."

A horse is said to be in the shoulder-in position when moving forward with his body in the same attitude as he would adopt following the pattern of a six-meter circle (volte). When the horse travels sideways on a tangent course, the horse will be crossing all four legs with greater emphasis on the crossing of the inside foreleg over the outside foreleg. The shoulder-in prepares the horse for collection because it flexes the inside loin muscles and engages the inside hindquarters.

The shoulder-in is a maneuver in which the rider brings the horse's shoulders toward the inside of the arena while maintaining the horse's posterior on the track. The horse's spinal column from croup to head must remain evenly bent at all times.

The shoulder-in should first be practiced at the walk and then at the slow trot and canter. At the canter, the shoulder-in is an exercise that will invite the horse to shift his weight on the haunches, which will be very beneficial when the study of flying changes of lead begins. The shoulder-in at the canter is a difficult movement that is not required in the F. E. I. competitions.

An important and noteworthy resource for any horseman's library is François Robichon de La Guérinière's *School of Horsemanship* [E*cole de Cavalerie Part II Complete Edition*, Xenophon Press 2015.]

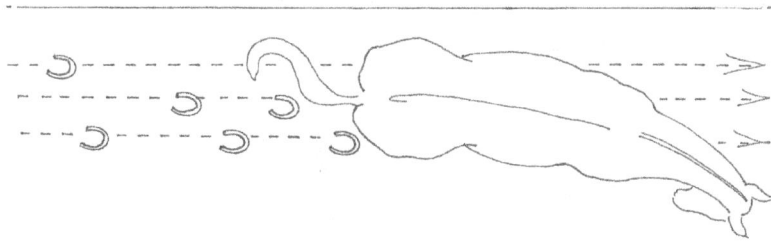

Figure 9 - Shoulder-in

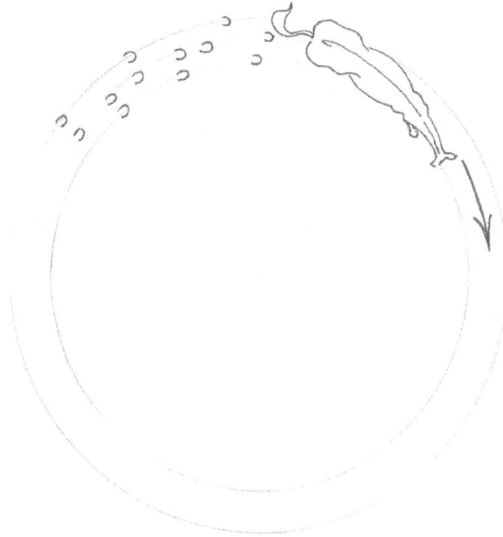

Figure 10 - Shoulder-in on circle

Goals of the Shoulder-In

1. To free the horse's inside shoulder: When the horse works with energy, the horse's inside anterior is compelled to produce a larger movement, flex at the knee and lift the shoulder to come in front and around the outside anterior.

2. To develop suppleness of the haunches: The inside hip is compelled to lower, which allows the same posterior to flex at the hock joint enabling the hind leg to engage and pass slightly in front of the outside hind leg. Engagement occurs when the horse's hind legs are stepping forward under the horse's body toward his center of gravity. Collection is the flexion of the loins that invites the hocks to flex. In the case of the shoulder-in, the horse is considered to be half-collected as the horse lowers his loins only on concave side.

3. To harmonize and connect both extremities of the horse's body from back to front: The shoulder-in supples the horse's entire spinal column by exercising the horse's top line muscles in all directions.

4. To develop the lateral flexion of the horse's neck and poll: When the horse's spine is bent, the stimulation of the rider's inside leg induces the lateral flexion of the poll around the first two vertebrae (atlas and axis).

5. To teach the horse to willingly submit to the rider's aids (obedience): The lateral action of the rider's leg and hand on the same side compel the horse to bend his spine and make it difficult for the horse to resist since the horse wants to avoid falling. The horse must submit to the rider's aids. (Viewed in this manner, the shoulder-in is equivalent to the arm block used in martial arts.)

6. To retrain the horse: If a rider works the horse in shoulder-in for a few days, the rider will restore full agility in the spoiled horse due to improper schooling. (Masters refer to the shoulder-in as the Aspirin of equitation.)

The shoulder-in should be practiced on both the right and left sides to develop suppleness over the horse's entire body. Difficulties can be overcome by gaining results on one side and without overdoing or sacrificing the other side.

Rider's Aids for the Right Shoulder-In *(It will be the opposite for the left shoulder-in.)*

Hands: The right indirect rein behind the withers, acting directly on the horse's center of gravity, solicits the horse's entire body to travel sideways to the left. The rider's hands should remain soft so that the horse stays light on the bit. The horse should yield laterally to the rein without leaning on the inside hand so that he can move laterally properly.

The left rein yields, allowing the action of the right rein and, if necessary, regulates it.

Legs: The right leg, acting at the girth, is the axis around which the horse bends his entire spine by withdrawing his coastal ribs to the left. The right leg maintains the engagement and the activity of the horse's inside posterior.

The left leg should be kept slightly behind the girth to prevent any eventual drifting of the horse's haunches to the left.

Seat: The rider's weight should be increased on the left seat bone and the left stirrup iron to incite the horse to displace his entire body toward the left. The rider's shoulders remain parallel to the horse's shoulders.

The pressure of the rider's inside leg at the girth is analogous to the action of a ballerina placing her hand at the waist to inflect the spinal column. The horse must learn to bend around the rider's inside leg. The rider should have the feeling that the horse is wrapping his body around the rider's inside leg at the girth while lowering his loins on the concave side. When the horse travels in this bent position, the rider's shoulders should remain in line and parallel with the horse's shoulders.

The rider's hands indicate the positioning, and the rider's legs produce the action. The lessons of the shoulder-in should be brief with the rider rewarding the horse often. In the shoulder-in, the horse moves in the opposite direction of the bend, i.e. for the shoulder-in to the right, the horse's body will be concave to the right as he moves to the left. The curvature of the spinal column should be as even as possible from tail to poll and moderate since the horse's body parts do not have equal flexibility. The horse will be looking in the direction from which he was coming while the tips of both of his ears should be kept level, without any head tilting.

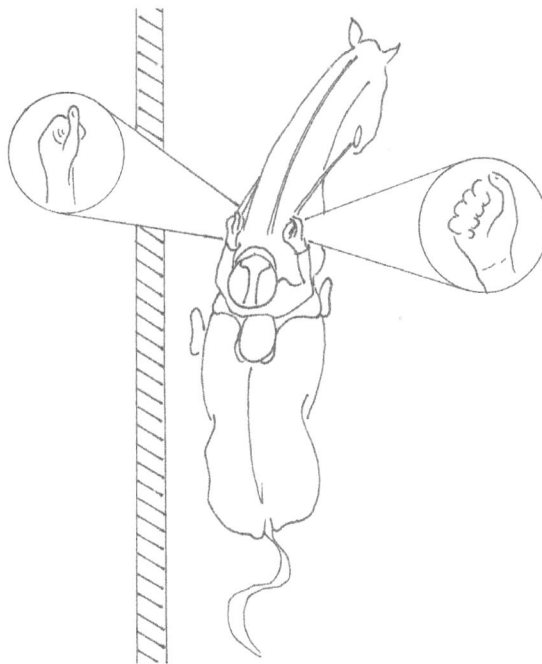

Figure 11 - Overall view of the aids for the Shoulder-in

Nota Bene

The rider's natural aids will induce the horse to move sideways and forward. The universal law of gravity states that the rider's center of gravity must move in the direction of the horse's movement. When the rider sits on the concave side (right) of the horse's back the movement will be diminished by restraining the action of the horse. This counter-sitting also interferes with the actions of the rider's right side. Sitting on the convex side (left) will automatically emphasize the movement by giving more freedom to the horse. A careful rider will be wary of a horse that may try to avoid bending and engaging his inside posterior by causing the rider to shift his/her weight to the wrong seat bone.

Shoulder-Fore

The shoulder-fore may be thought of as a half shoulder-in. Europeans from north of the Rhine River have never really accepted the concept of the shoulder-in, but have, instead, adopted a practice of reducing the angle of the shoulder-in.

The French School defines the shoulder-in *(épaule en dedans)* as the shoulder-inside; the horse's body is positioned at a 30 to 35 degree angle to the path of travel. The German School defines the shoulder-fore *(Schulter vör)* as the shoulder ahead in which the horse's body is positioned at a 10 to 15 degree angle to the path of travel.

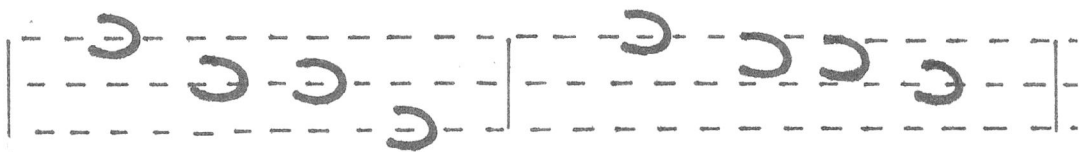

Figure 12 -   *Shoulder-in*   *Shoulder-fore*

What is the difference between a three-track and four-track shoulder-in?

The horse can travel in the shoulder-in on either three or four tracks. When the horse travels on three parallel and equidistant tracks, the horse's inside shoulder is obliged to lift the inside fore knee to overlap the outside foreleg and he simultaneously lowers his inside haunch and engages this posterior forward and inward in the direction of the opposite anterior, thereby oscillating toward the medial plane of his center of gravity.

When the horse travels on four parallel and equidistant tracks, the inside shoulder emphasizes the lifting of the inside fore knee that urges the horse to lower the inside haunch. The horse's posterior on the same side will overlap in front of the outside posterior, but not toward the horse's center of gravity. The horse will not engage under his center of gravity, but will propel himself forward by virtue of the crossing.

It may be beneficial for some horses to practice the shoulder-in on three tracks. As the horse begins to develop suppleness, the work on four tracks will help unlock the abductor and adductor muscles and improve the flexibility of the hock joints. Ultimately, the work on four tracks will enable the horse perform the work on three tracks with greater ease, which is required in dressage competitions.

How does the rider teach the shoulder-in?

Before teaching the shoulder-in, the rider must fulfill the following prerequisites:

1. The rider must be well-accomplished (without any hesitation) in the aids of the shoulder-in and understand why they are used.

2. The horse must be obedient to the rider's hands. The horse should respond to any hand action of the direct and indirect rein and easily displace his shoulders in any direction.

3. The horse must be obedient to the rider's leg actions at the girth and behind the girth. With the active leg at the girth, the rider should be able to bend the horse's body. When the rider's leg is acting behind the girth, the horse should displace his haunches in either direction. The rider should also be able to prohibit the haunches from moving if the horse has taken an evasive initiative.

4. The horse must be obedient to the simultaneous actions of the rider's legs and hand. For example, when tracking right on a small circle, the rider acts with the right indirect rein and a right leg at the girth, the horse's body should be easily displaced sideways toward the left onto a larger circle and vice versa when tracking left (cession to the leg).

Two Progressive Methods to Teach the Shoulder-in, tracking right
(It will be the opposite for the shoulder-in tracking to the left.)

Method One:

Tracking left, at the beginning of the long side of the manège on an inside track about 4 to 6 feet parallel to the wall, the rider applies a right direct rein to lead the horse to the right toward the wall. Following the wall, the rider then acts with a right indirect rein behind the withers with the right leg at the girth to maintain the horse's body in a consistent bend. After traveling a few steps in this semblance of a shoulder-in [right] position, the rider will move the right hand slightly forward and to the left to straighten the horse's body by pushing the horse's shoulder to the left onto an inside track and then animate the pace to recreate the activity of the posteriors. Repeating the same exercise several times teaches the horse to maintain the shoulder-in in reverse (also known as the counter shoulder-in or shoulder-out) without too much stress and effort.

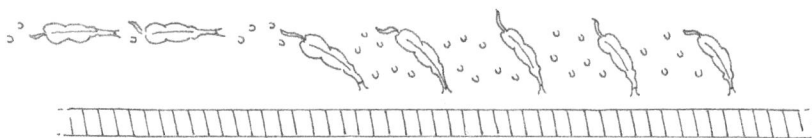

Shoulder-out near the wall.

Shoulder-out away from the wall.

Figure 13 - Shoulder-out

The rider should repeat the same exercise about 8-10 feet from the wall to make certain that the horse remains on the new parallel course. If the horse has a slight tendency to return to the wall, the rider should regulate this evasion by acing and resisting (half-parade) using a left direct rein of opposition.

Method Two:

Tracking right at the beginning of the long side of the arena, the rider leads the horse onto a small 6-8 meter circle (volte) tangent to the track to invite the horse to bend his spine. At the end of this circle, the rider should immediately begin a second revolution. Then the rider should shift his/her weight onto the left stirrup and simultaneously apply a soft right indirect rein of opposition behind the withers and the right leg at the girth. These aids should be applied with firm but gentle authority similar to that of a dancer's arm leading his partner. This second circle is the prelude to the shoulder-in.

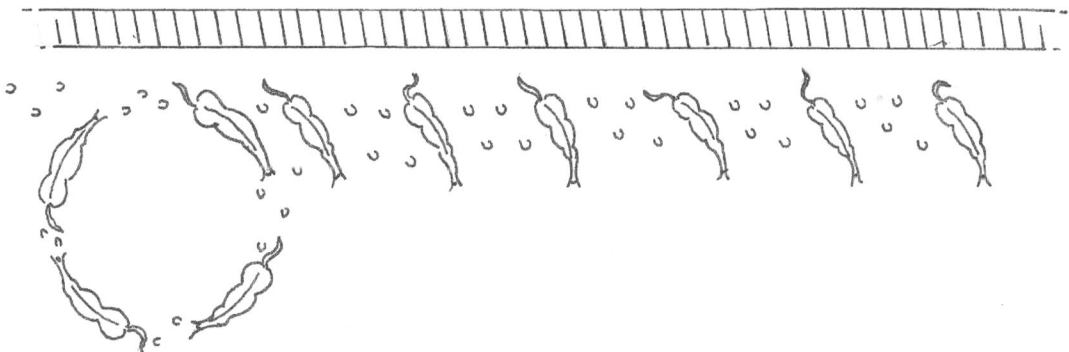

Figure 14 - Shoulder-in using circles; straight

At this stage of the dressage, the rider's goal should be the idea of the movement without as much concern for accuracy. Perfection will come later as the horse becomes more familiar with the exercise. After a few steps in the shoulder-in, the rider should begin another small circle to the right to restore straightness as well as the activity of the posteriors, and then begin the same exercise again. After several days of practice, the rider should be able to maintain the shoulder-in for a few more steps and gradually encounter less resistance from the horse. With continued careful practice, the rider should be able to begin a shoulder-in by simply leading the horse's anterior onto an inside track using a quarter of a volte. When the horse is accustomed to this new work at the walk, the rider can begin the same progression in the trot and then at the canter.

Faults to Avoid

1. An accentuated bend in the horse's neck will incite the horse to fall on his outside shoulder (opposite side of the bend) and the anteriors will likely veer back to the original track. The horse's spine should maintain an even, regular bend like a croissant au beurre and not like the Bishop's croissier.

2. If the angle to the path of travel is too great in the shoulder-in, the horse will be compelled to lower his withers.

3. If the rider displaces the weight distribution counter to the direction of travel, the horse's lateral movement will diminish. The rider's weight should always be in the direction of the motion. In the shoulder-in to the right, the horse will be traveling to the left; therefore, the rider's weight should be shifted to the left.

Troubleshooting

Problem: In performing the shoulder-in, the horse tries to leave the track and turns toward the inside of the arena.

Solution: The lack of activity of the inside posterior does not support the horse and will result in the haunches deviating to the right, inciting the horse to fall toward the right inside. To correct this problem, the rider should reconfirm the action of the inside leg at the girth and slightly reinforce the action of her outside leg behind the girth. The rider should apply the right indirect rein of opposition behind the withers with slightly more determination to maintain the horse on the track. The rider may also gently act, resist and release using the outside direct rein of opposition to prevent the horse from leaving the track (half-parade).

Problem: The horse does not maintain the bend and wants to straighten his body.

Solution: The horse's spine may still be too rigid to perform the shoulder-in. The rider should use patterns of half-circles and full circles and gradually tightening the serpentines to stretch and supple the horse's spine *(see Divide and Conquer Book 1)*. To maintain the horse on three equidistant tracks, the rider should be vigilant in coordinating the action and reaction of the hands and legs to compel the horse's shoulder and haunches to stay in line.

Problem: The horse falls on his outside shoulder.

Solution: When the horse falls on his outside shoulder, it can be the result of a lack of activity of the horse's inside posterior. If the rider over bends the horse's neck, of course, the horse will also fall on the outside shoulder. The rider should accentuate the action of the inside leg at the girth to oblige the horse to react by instinct to conserve his energy and maintain the proper bend. By alternating tight circles with straight lines, the rider can incite the horse to become more active with his posterior legs.

Problem: The horse shows difficulties crossing his inside posterior over the outside posterior.

Solution: The rider should decrease the angle of the shoulder-in from a 30 degree angle to the track to a 15 degree angle and activate the inside posterior with more determination. The rider should also review the rotation of the shoulders around the haunches, i.e. pirouettes and the rotation of the haunches around the shoulder, i.e. counter pirouette, to correct the problem.

Problem: The horse twists his head and neck to the opposite side (one ear stands lower than the other).

Solution: The horse is maintaining proper equilibrium when a line drawn through the tips of the ears remains parallel to the ground. Tilting of the horse's head indicates that the horse has lost impulsion and is no longer equally connected on the two reins, which is usually the result of the rider's excess strength of one of the hands, usually the outside hand. The rider should soften the outside rein without reinforcing the action of the inside rein. If brief and repeated rotations of the outside wrist (supination) do not correct the problem, the rider should leave the shoulder-in exercise and stimulate the horse forward on a straight line until the neck and head are again in line. The reins should provide symmetrical contact with the horse's mouth so that the top of the horse's ears remain parallel with the ground without the horse favoring one side of his neck over the other.

Problem: The horse resists the rider's hand.

Solution: The horse's resistance to the rider's hand results from too great a bend, causing the horse to fall on his outside shoulder due to a distinct lack of engagement of the inside posterior. To compensate, the horse will displace his haunches to the outside. To correct the problem, the rider should reduce the horse's bend by lightening the action of the inside rein and regulating a little more with the outside hand.

Problem: The horse is resistant to the exercise.

Solution: The rider has overworked the horse so that he cannot perform the exercise any longer.

During training sessions, the rider should interrupt any given exercise often and send the horse forward as well as provide him a rest period. Ceasing the work/study for that day may also be a very wise idea. Often horses perform better on following days.

Nota Bene

The shoulder-in is the most difficult exercise to perform correctly, but it is the most useful of all the lateral movements. The rider should progress slowly in teaching the horse and should conscientiously practice softening the horse's mouth (cession of the jaws). If the horses gives much resistance, the rider should halt the horse in the shoulder-in position and negotiate a cession of the mouth before recommencing the exercise.

When the shoulder-in is practiced in reverse, i.e. tracking left with the horse's spine concave to the right, the movement is called counter shoulder-in, shoulder-in in reverse, or simply shoulder-out. The goal of this exercise is to incite the horse to exert more energy using his outside lateral biped.

Manège figures to improve the horse's flexibility in performing the Shoulder-In

Perform a figure eight, changing from shoulder-in to shoulder-out.

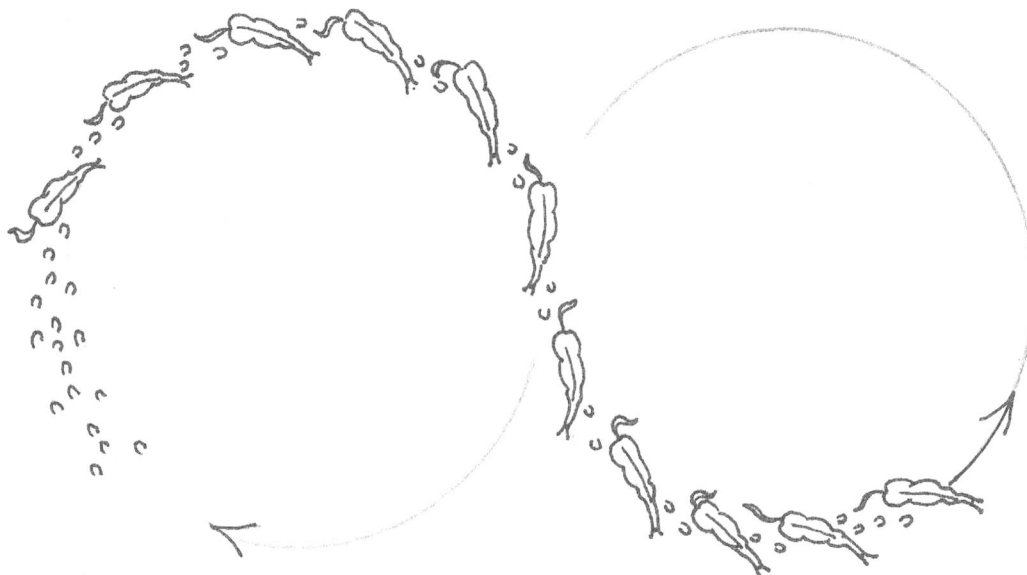

Figure 15 - Figure 8 shoulder-in to shoulder-out

Shoulder-in transitions between gaits or within the same gait are wonderful exercises to confirm the horse's obedience to the rider's aids. These transitions also amplify the effort of the horse's inside posterior to better engage and enhance the flexibility of the horse's spine.

Suggestions by Great Masters

When performing the shoulder-in at the trot, the rider should practice at slow pace and remain sitting in the saddle.

When the shoulder-in is practiced at the posting trot traveling to the right, the rider should rise with the left diagonal biped to better engage the right posterior and allow more freedom for a young horse. (It would be the opposite when traveling to the left.)

Either method can be used; it is only a matter of preference to ease the horse's efforts.

When the lesson of the shoulder-in has been well-executed on circles, and the horse has developed equal flexibility on both sides, the lesson should be performed on a straight line at the walk, then at the trot, and finally at the canter.

Historical anecdote

When the lesson of the shoulder-in was first introduced by Monsieur de La Guérinière, some young noblemen, who sought excuses to engage in dueling swords among themselves, used the new exercise to create conflicts. These horsemen annoyed each other by stating with exaggerated snobbish tones as if they had hot potatoes in their mouths,

"*Monsieur, mon ami*, from what I can observe, your horse is certainly not in a shoulder-in, but, indeed, he is in a dreadful haunches-out."

In becoming aware of these quarrels about the misconception of this teaching, Monsieur de La Guérinière, with great clarity, explained,

"Young gentlemen, you should understand that when you think that your horse is performing a shoulder-in at a walk, why don't you ask for a canter departure? If your horse strikes off on the good lead, you were, in fact, performing a correct shoulder-in. But if your horse gives you the wrong lead, you were, unfortunately, in a haunches-out and therefore, not in a shoulder-in."

CHAPTER THREE

Half-Pass (Appuyer)

A horse is said to be moving in half-pass when traveling laterally parallel to himself in which the anterior and posterior legs are on two different tracks. The horse looks in the direction of the movement with his head, neck and shoulders slightly preceding his haunches. The horse travels in the direction of the bend, i.e., the horse will be bending to the right when he is traveling to the right, and vice versa.

Figure 16 - Half-pass

Goals of the Half-Pass

1. To compel the horse to cross his posteriors to a greater degree than in the shoulder-in at the walk and trot.

2. To bring the two lateral bipeds closer, thereby reducing the polygon of sustentation.

3. To increase flexibility of the horse's loins.

Rider's Aids for the Half-Pass, traveling to the right (It will be the opposite traveling to the left.)

Hands: The rider's right hand acts with the direct rein to lead the horse and to maintain the position of the horse's nose in the direction of the motion. The rider's left hand yields to allow the action of the right hand and may, if necessary, act with a tactful indirect rein in front of the withers to solicit the horse's shoulders to move to the right.

Legs: The rider's right leg acts at the girth to slightly bend the horse's torso and maintain the activity. The rider's left leg acts behind the girth to propel the haunches to the right.

Seat: The rider's body should have more weight on the right stirrup to increase the weight on the right seat bone.

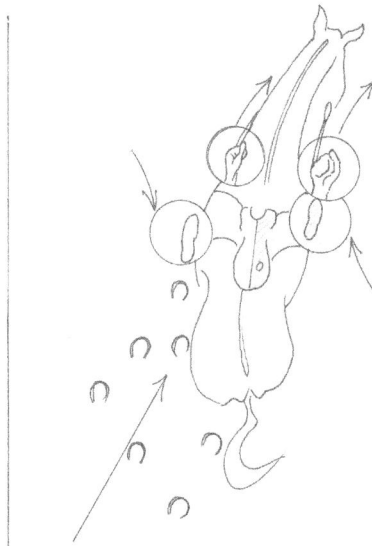

Figure 17 - Aids for half-pass

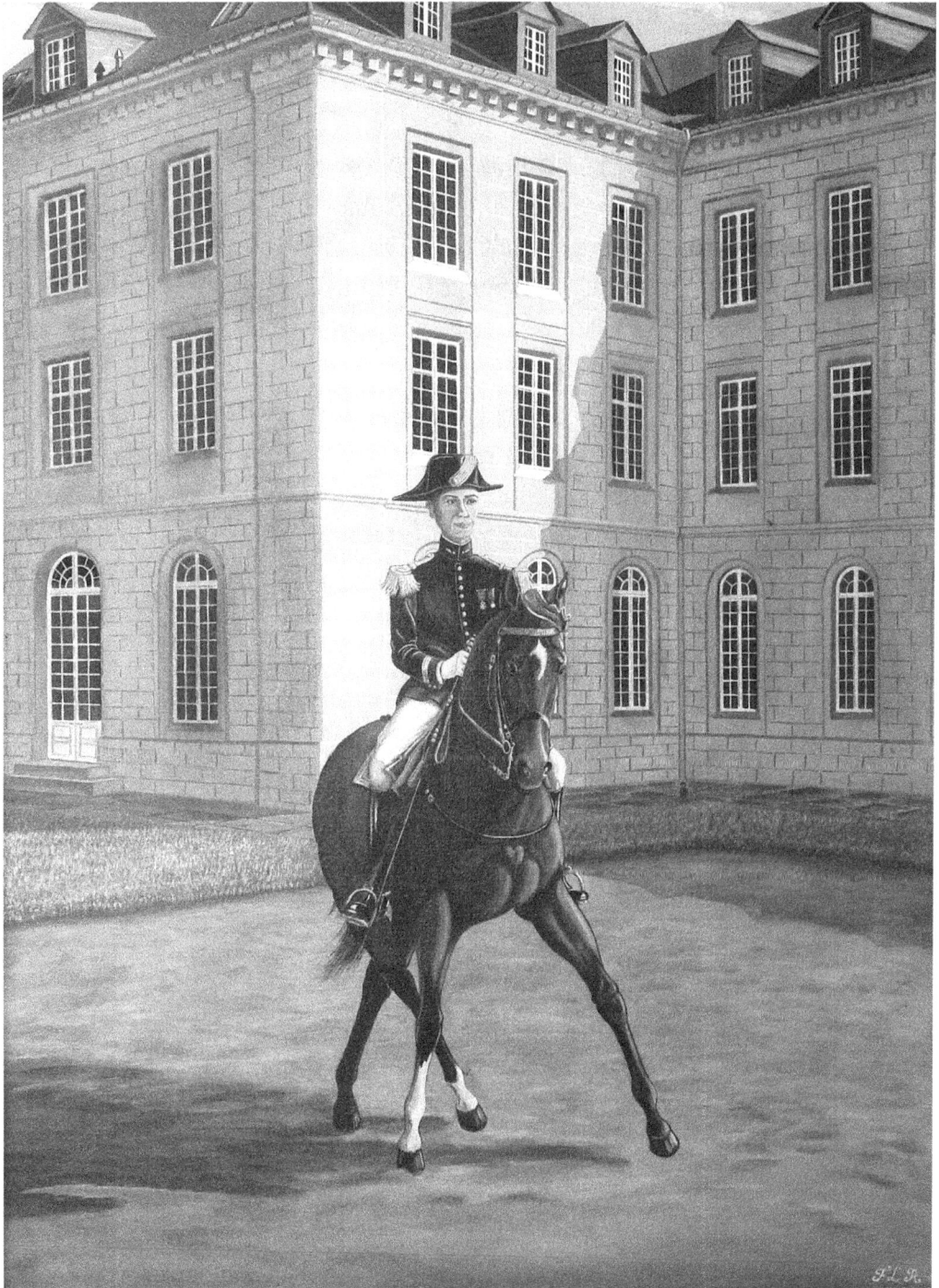

Plate 1: Half-pass in the Iéna carrière in Saumur. Painting by François Lemaire de Ruffieu

Teaching the Horse the Half-Pass, traveling to the right

(It will be the opposite traveling to the left.)

Work-study:

1. From a large circle of 15-20 meters in diameter tracking to the right, the rider will ask for a few steps in the shoulder-in and then straighten the horse's body. Next she will bring the horse's haunches toward the inside of the circle for a few steps. The rider should repeat this simple exercises several times in succession until the horse can easily and independently displace his forehand and haunches.

2. Traveling on the same large circle, the rider will try to simultaneously bring the horse's shoulders and the haunches toward the inside to obtain an even body bend. The rider should then spiral in to bring the horse's body closer to the center of the circle by acting with a right direct rein to lead the horse's forehand and simultaneously act with the left leg behind the girth to stimulate the haunches to the right. The rider's right leg remains at the girth to assist the bend and the impulsion.

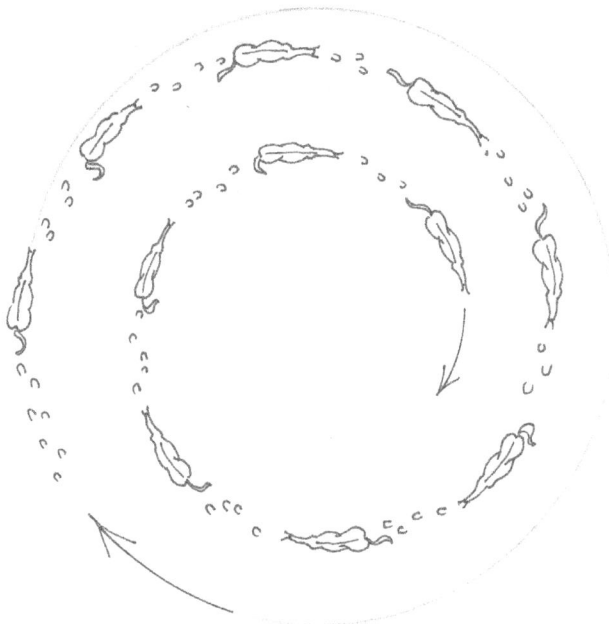

Figure 18 - Spiral towards the center of the circle

3. When the rider reaches the center of the circle, she should stimulate the horse forward and leave the circle on a straight line. Repeating this exercise several times will teach the horse to displace his entire body sideways.

Even though the horse will lose amplification of the stride in the first steps of the half-pass, it is preferable to begin the half-pass with a few steps in the shoulder-in so that the horse will not begin the half-pass with his haunches leading.

Nota Bene

As the horse improves the execution of the half-pass, the rider's aids should be simplified. For a half-pass to the right, the rider will simply use a direct rein associated with the left leg behind the girth. It will be the opposite for a half-pass to the left.

Mistakes to Avoid

If the rider proceeds into the half-pass by pushing the horse's shoulders with an outside indirect rein, she will block the horse's outside shoulder and lose the amplitude of the movement.

If the rider proceeds into the half-pass by acting with a right indirect rein to maintain the horse's nose in the direction of the motion, she will burden and obstruct the horse's right shoulder and may incite the horse to veer to the left.

Exercises to Develop and Improve the Half-Pass

1. Following the pattern of a wide half-volte, the rider will ask her horse to maintain the haunches toward the inside for half the circle and then apply the aids of the half-pass on the oblique line returning to the track.

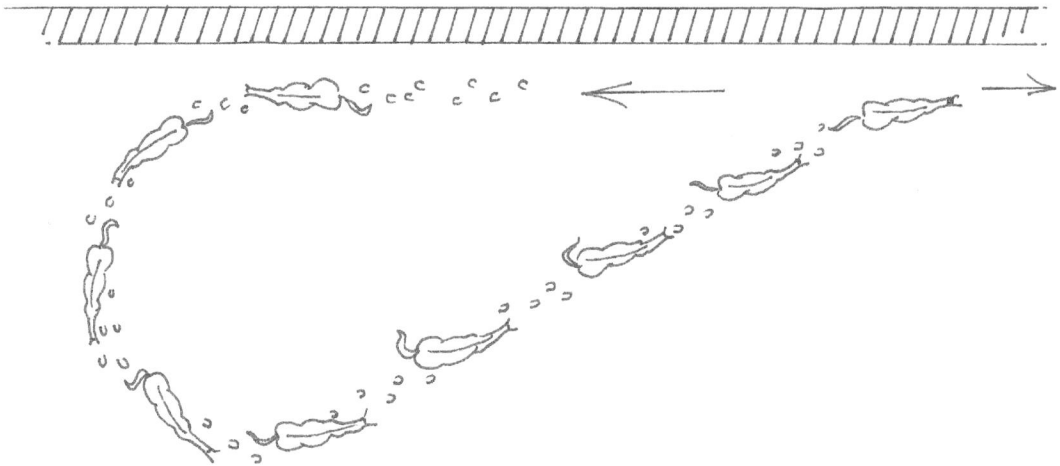

Figure 19 - Half-volte to half-pass

2. Following the pattern of a counter-change of direction (zigzag), the rider will apply the aids of the half-pass for a few steps toward the inside of the arena, then maintain the horse on a brief straight line between the two opposite oblique lines before returning to the track with a half-pass toward the outside.

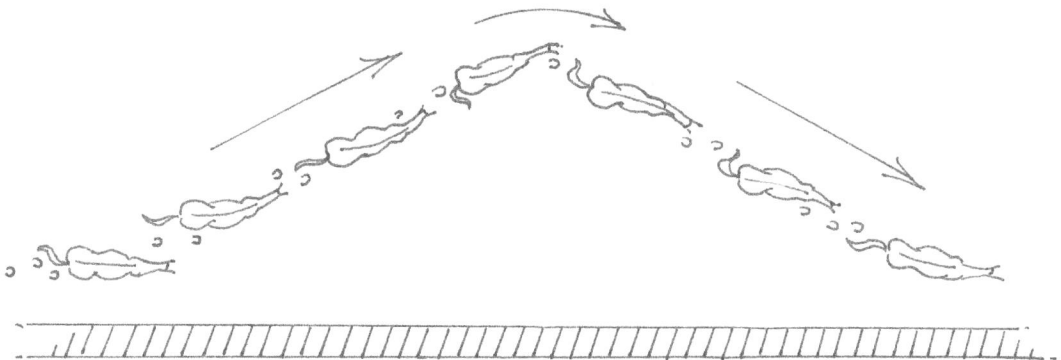

Figure 20 - Counter-change of direction and half-pass

3. Staircase Exercise. On the diagonal of the arena, the rider should practice alternating a few steps of half-pass traveling sideways with a few steps of the shoulder-in traveling on a straight line parallel to the track. The pair should continue sideways and straight in the same manner to the opposite end of the diagonal of the arena.

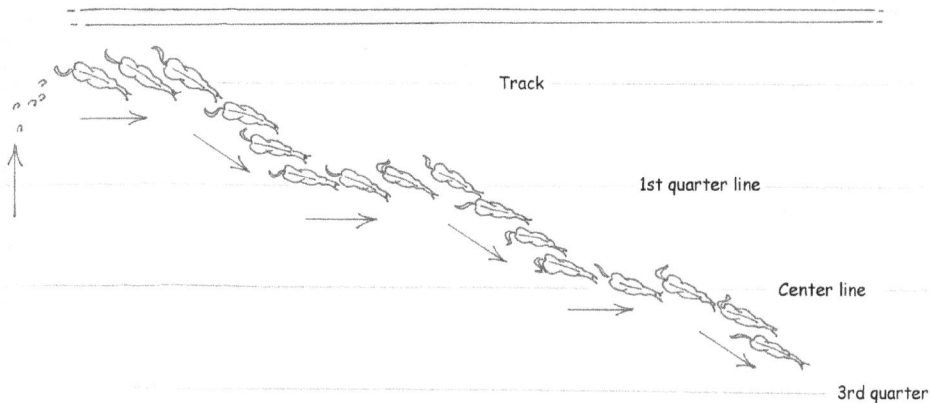

Figure 21 - Staircase

4. In the middle of the diagonal at the center of the arena, the rider should interrupt the half-pass with a half rotation around the haunches (similar to a half-pirouette) to return to the starting corner of the arena.

In the middle of the diagonal, the rider should interrupt the half-pass with a half rotation around the shoulders (similar to a counter-pirouette) and return to the starting corner.

When the horse is more supple, the rider may ask for a complete rotation around the haunches or the shoulders and continue in the original direction to complete the diagonal.

Figure 22 - Half and complete rotation around the haunches

41

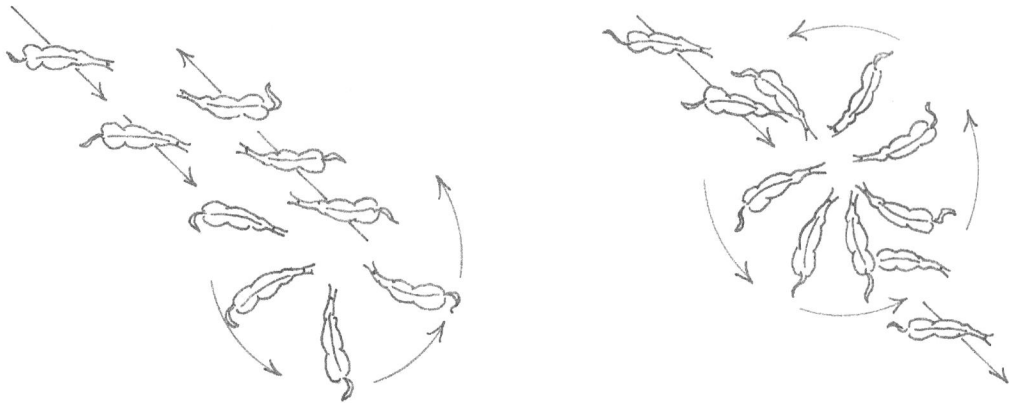

Figure 23 - Half-pass to 1/2 counter-pirouette, full pirouette

5. On a circle, the rider will perform the half-pass with the shoulders and the haunches inside the circle or outside the circle.

Figure 24 - Half-pass haunches-out, haunches-in on circle

6. On a straight line and on a circle the rider should switch from a half-pass to the left to a half-pass to the right or vice versa in a zigzag pattern (counter-changes).

7. While maintaining the horse in half-pass, the rider will perform upward and downward transitions within the same gait on a straight line and later on a circle.

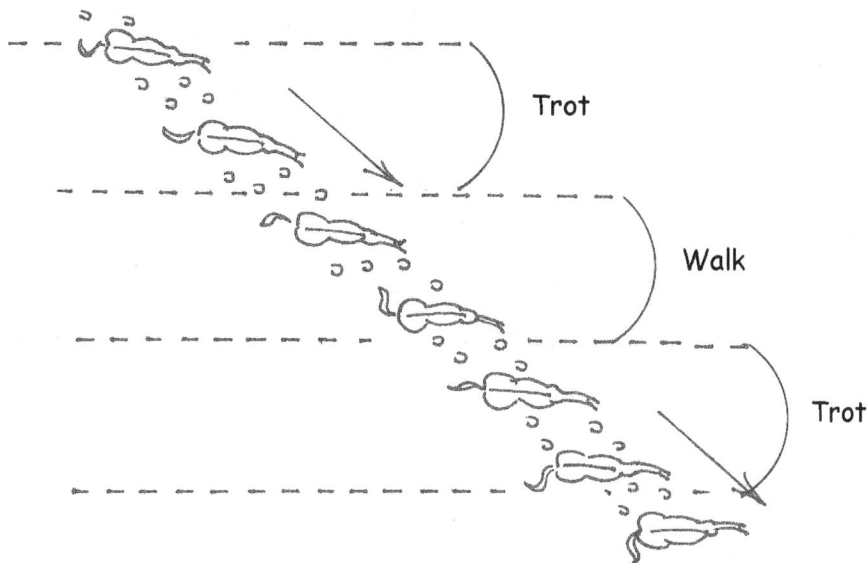

Figure 25 - Transitions in the half-pass

Nota Bene

In the early stages of learning the half-pass, the horse may have difficulty crossing his legs. The rider could demand a slight angle of 20 to 25 degrees between the horse's body and the direction of the motion. If the horse exaggerates the crossing of legs and slows the pace, the rider should straighten the horse's body for a few strides and restart the half-pass.

At the walk, the horse should perform equal crossing of the anterior and posterior limbs. At the trot, the horse may show greater crossing of the anteriors. At the canter, crossing of the limbs is almost nonexistent. In theory, the horse should be able to move the posteriors easier than the anteriors. When performing the half-pass on a circle, if the horse's haunches are to the inside, the displacement of the posteriors will be reduced compared to the anteriors since the horse will be covering more ground with the anterior portion of his body. The opposite would occur when performing a half-pass on a circle with the haunches toward to the outside.

At the trot, if the horse has difficulty traveling sideways with the rider sitting the trot, the rider should post on the leading diagonal to incite the

43

outside posterior to engage better, i.e. for a half-pass to the right, the rider should rise to the trot on the right diagonal biped and vice versa when traveling left. Always remember that forward motion is a higher priority than lateral displacement.

Troubleshooting (The following solutions are for a half-pass to the right. It will be the opposite when traveling left.)

Problem: The horse falls to the right or exaggerates the sideways movement.

Solution: The rider should increase the impulsion with the right leg at the girth and/or travel on a straight line for a few strides before demanding the half-pass again.

Problem: The horse travels more forward than sideways to the right.

Solution: The rider should reduce the speed and insist on acting with the proper aids for the half-pass and maintaining the right leg at the girth.

Problem: The horse leads too much with his forehand.

Solution: When the horse leads too much with his shoulders, the horse tends to straighten his body and sacrifice the bend. The rider should emphasize the action of the inside leg at the girth and the outside leg behind (or slightly behind) the girth to maintain the bend. By using the hands to correct the problem, the rider would block the horse, causing the horse to create too much bend in the neck and lose amplification of the motion. To regain the bend of the horse's body, the rider should begin again with a volte.

Problem: The horse leads with his haunches.

Solution: A horse that leads with his haunches shows clear signs of lack of synchronization of his legs and is moving on his forehand, usually as a result of the rider applying too much action with the outside leg behind the girth. Instead, the rider should reinforce the action of the inside leg at the girth and reposition the shoulders in front of the haunches using a direct rein on the right.

Problem: The horse slows the pace.

Solution: When the horse slows the pace, he shortens his strides and is not able to travel sideways. The movement becomes irregular and the horse no longer propels himself. To remedy this problem, the rider should act with the legs to stimulate the gait or depart the exercises to a more forward pace. If the rider feels the horse might be tiring, discontinue the exercise and give the horse a deserved rest. A horse should not slow the pace without command by the rider.

Problem: The horse breaks into a canter.

Solution: A horse that breaks into a canter indicates a lack of engagement of the inside posterior. The problem must be solved in the forward motion. If the horse breaks into a canter, the rider should maintain the half-pass in the canter for a few strides and return to a more forward trot. Then begin the study of the half-pass again at the trot but at a slower pace.

Nota Bene

The amplification of the horse's strides depends on the horse's level of dressage education, his suppleness, relaxation, and the angle of the half-pass.

While performing the half-pass, the rider should remember that if the horse is leading with his shoulders too much, the horse is NOT YET in the half-pass. If the horse is leading with his haunches, the horse is NO LONGER in the half-pass.

Most horses show more difficulty performing half-pass to the right than the left because of their inborn body curvature. A subtle and progressive training method should eliminate this difference.

Complementary Lateral Exercises to Improve Shoulder-In and Half-Pass

Haunches-In (Travers) and Haunches-Out (Renvers)

A horse is said to be in a haunches-in position when moving forward with his body posture in the same position as that of a volte (6-8 meter circle). For a haunches-in tracking right, the horse's body will be in a concave position toward the inside of the track (the right). The horse should be looking in the direction that he is traveling. The haunches will be displaced to the inside of the path of the shoulders so that the outside posterior slightly crosses over the inside posterior. In the haunches-out, the horse's concavity would be opposite.

Figure 26 - Haunches-in, straight, haunches-out

Goals for the Haunches-in

1. To teach the horse to better cross the posteriors.

2. Provide suppleness to the muscles in the spinal region.

3. Develop power in the haunches, stifles, and loins area.

4. Perfect the lateral bending.

5. Invite the horse to give cession of the mouth.

Rider's aids for Haunches-In when tracking to the right

(The opposite aids will be used when tracking left.)

Hands: The right hand acts with a soft indirect rein of opposition in front of the withers to place the horse's nose toward the direction of the motion.

The left hand yields to allow the action of the right hand and then regulates this action if necessary.

Legs: The right leg acts at the girth to maintain the bend and the activity of the inside posterior.

The left leg acts behind the girth to solicit the horse to move his haunches to the right.

Seat: The rider should discreetly increase the weight on the right seat bone and the right stirrup.

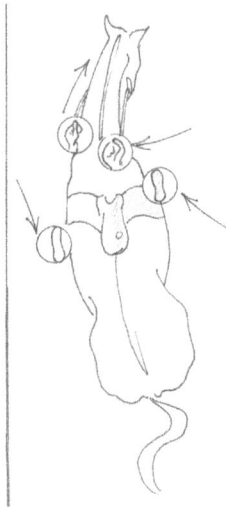

Figure 27 - Aids for the haunches-in and haunches-out

Teaching the horse Haunches-In when tracking to the right

Tracking right, beginning of the long side of the arena in a volte (6-8 meter circle) tangent to the track, the rider should sustain a bend in the horse's body to the right by maintaining the right leg at the girth and the left leg behind the girth.

When the horse's forehand reaches the end of the circle, which is at the long side of the arena, the rider should shift her weight toward the right and simultaneously apply a soft right indirect rein in front of the withers and a left leg behind the girth. After a few steps of traveling sideways, the rider should begin another circle to return to single track work (without crossing), reanimate the gait, and begin the exercise again. Over a period of time, the rider should gradually increase the number of steps of sideways traveling.

Troubleshooting

Problem: The horse has difficulty maintaining his haunches on an inside track

Solution: Horses will always encounter greater difficulties in crossing their posteriors than their anteriors. From the ground, the rider should review the cession of the legs lesson described in Divide and Conquer Book 1. While mounted, the rider should repeat the same lesson with the aid of a Gentle Helper on the ground to encourage the displacement of the haunches. When the horse displaces his haunches with ease and without hesitation, the rider may begin again practicing the lessons.

Figure 28 - Using the whip in hand

Problem: The horse moves his haunches more than his shoulders and tends to turn around on his forehand.

Solution: The rider should slow the pace and allow the horse to learn the movement. The rider may increase the action of her right leg at the girth to stimulate the horse's right posterior. The rider should act with a discrete left indirect rein to stimulate the shoulders to move toward the right without losing the bend.

Problem: The rider is falling on the left seat bone.

Solution: To help the horse travel with freedom, the rider should increase the weight on the right seat bone. If the horse manages to shift the rider's weight onto the side opposite the direction of travel (and bend), the rider should lean forward slightly to lighten the weight on the horse's haunches and increase the weight on the right stirrup.

Exercises to improve the Haunches-in when traveling to the right
(Perform the exercises in the opposite manner when traveling left.)

1. Practice the study of the horse's rotation of the hind legs around the forelegs (counter pirouette).

2. On a 15-meter circle, maintain the haunches to the inside the circle. Repeat the same circle with the haunches maintained toward the outside and alternate again with the haunches toward the inside of the circle.

3. Traveling on an inside track parallel to the wall, the rider should maintain the horse's haunches toward the inside and, as a separate exercise, to the outside.

4. Ride transitions on circles and straight lines with the haunches-in toward the inside of the circle.

5. Ride a serpentine pattern, and alternately maintain the horse in shoulder-in and then in haunches-in on the various loops.

6. Ride the pattern of a figure eight and maintain the horse in shoulder-in for the first half-circle and then change to a haunches-in for the second circle (in the opposite direction) then return to shoulder-in for the last half-circle to complete the figure eight.

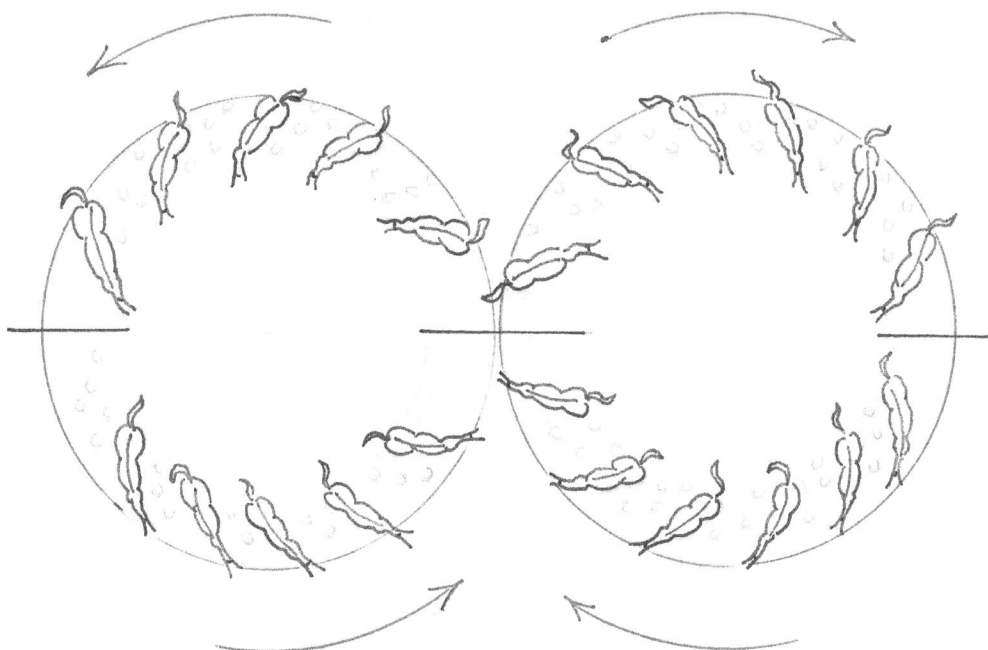

Figure 29 - Figure 8, shoulder-in, haunches-in

Nota Bene

The haunches-in and the half-pass are similar exercises. When the haunches-in exercise is performed on the diagonal, it is referred to as a half-pass. When it is performed on a straight line, it is called the haunches-in or travers.

Head to the Wall

The horse is said to be in a head to the wall position when following the track around the arena with his head close to the wall. His anterior will be on the track while his posterior on an inside track. The horse should maintain a slight bend between 45 and 80 degrees, depending on the horse's abilities, with the concavity toward the direction of the movement. The head to the wall is an exaggeration of the haunches-in.

Because of the lack of open space in front of the horse, the rider may experience a reduction in the horse's activity and diminishing forward motion. The horse may also develop the tendency to allow the wall to guide him instead of being attentive to the rider's aids. Despite these disadvantages, the use of the wall as a temporary aid will allow the rider and the horse to clearly understand the exercise.

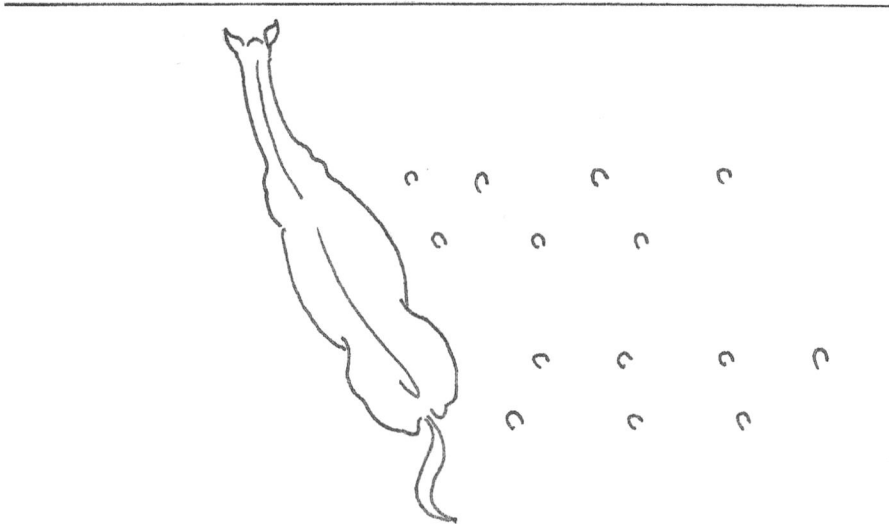

Figure 30 - Head to the wall

Goals of the Head to the Wall Exercise

1. Develop mobility to improve crossing of the anteriors especially on the convex side.

2. Stretch the spinal muscles (psoas) on the convex side and add flexibility to the spinal muscles on the concave side.

3. Confirm the horse's obedience to the rider's inside leg at the girth.

4. Prepares the horse for half-pass and pirouette.

Rider's Aids for Head to the Wall

The following aids are for a horse tracking to the right. (They will be the opposite when tracking to the left.)

The rider will be traveling right on an inside track parallel to the wall about four feet in from the normal track.

Hands: The rider's left hand acts with a direct rein to lead the horse toward the wall and to maintain the horse's nose to the left. When the horse reaches the wall, the rider will switch the direct rein to an indirect rein to push the horse's shoulders to the right while maintaining the nose to the left.

Legs: The rider's left leg acts at the girth to maintain the bend and the impulsion;

The rider's right leg acts behind the girth to bring and maintain the horse's haunches on an inside track.

Seat: The rider's weight should be increased on the right seat bone and the right stirrup.

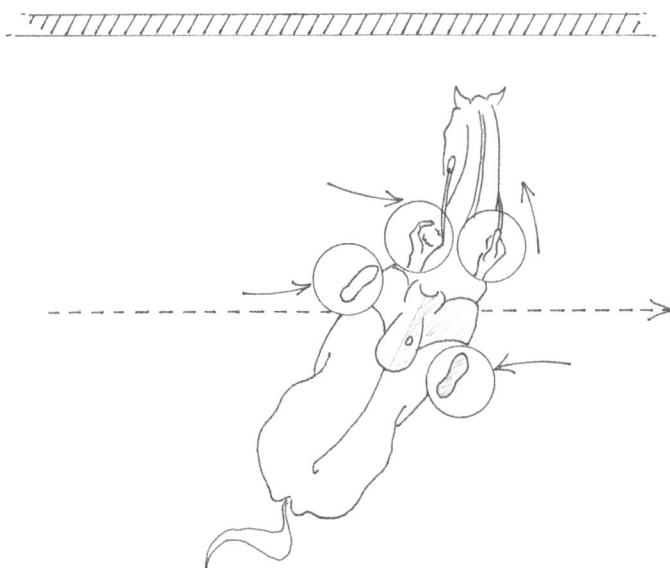

Figure 31 - Aids for head to the wall

Troubleshooting

Problem: The horse has difficult traveling sideways at an angle of 80 degrees.

Solution: If the horse shows difficulty in bending at an 80 degree angle, it usually means that the horse is not yet ready for the exercise. The rider should proceed gradually from an angle of 35 degrees to reach an angle of 55 degrees over a long enough period of time to generate suppleness in the horse's spine. Review of the pirouette and counter pirouette exercises will also help to provide suppleness of the horse's spine and limbs.

Problem: The horse travels too fast.

Solution: In traveling too fast, the horse is trying to avoid the exercise by shortening his strides and/or running. The rider should proceed slowly without demanding too much from the horse. The rider's patience will be rewarded with the horse's gradual improvement.

Problem: The horse travels too slowly.

Solution: When the horse travels too slowly, it is the result of a lack of activity of the posteriors. Traveling on straight lines and in circles, the rider should review the upward transitions from one gait to another as well as rotation of the shoulders around the haunches and the haunches around the shoulders.

Croup to the Wall

In the croup to the wall exercise, the horse follows the enclosure of the arena with his croup being close to the wall with the posteriors on the track and the anteriors on an inside track, forming a body angle between 45 and 80 degrees. Tracking right, the horse will be bent to the left; vice versa for the horse tracking left.

The croup to the wall exercise is a variant of the half-pass. The wall provides the novice horse with a guideline to follow and maintain the correct path and because of the open space in front of the horse, the horse's activity is better maintained. Tracking right, the horse will be bent to the left, and vice versa when tracking to the left.

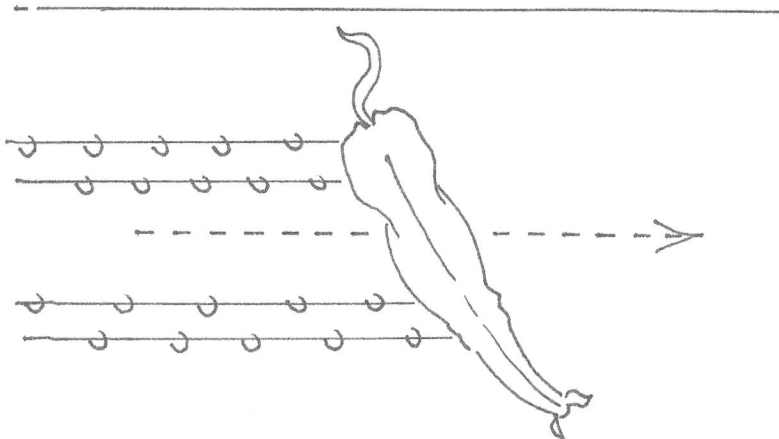

Figure 32 - Croup to the wall

Goals of the Croup to the Wall

1. To develop the agility of the hind legs the exercise enables the crossing, especially the posterior on the convex side.

2. The exercise stretches the spinal column on the convex side and loosens the muscles on the concave side.

3. The exercise provides conditioning for the horse that has a tendency to neglect the bend while performing the half-pass.

Rider's Aids for the Croup to the Wall

The rider will be traveling right on an inside track about 4 feet parallel to the normal track. *(The opposite aids are used when tracking to the left.)*

Hands: The rider's left hand acts with a direct rein to lead and place the horse's nose in the direction of the motion.

The rider's right hand yields and then regulates the action of the left hand.

Legs: The rider's left leg should act at the girth to bend the horse's spine to the left and maintain the impulsion.

The rider's right leg should act behind the girth to stimulate the horse's haunches to the left.

Seat: The rider's weight should be increased on the left seat bone and the left stirrup.

Note: Tracking right, the horse's body will be bent to the left (it will be bent right when tracking left).

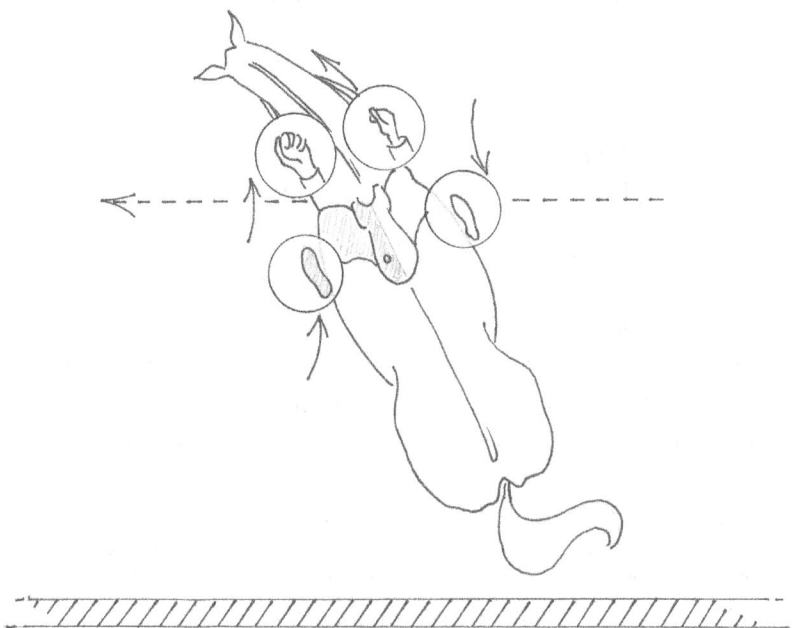

Figure 33 - Aids for croup to the wall

Troubleshooting

Problem: The horse has difficulty traveling at a steep angle.

Solution: Progressing gradually from a wide angle to smaller angle over a period of time will enable the horse to develop suppleness and agility. The limbs on the concave and convex sides must be suppled so that they can stretch and cross, making the sideways displacement possible.

Problem: The horse attempts to rush the exercise.

Solution: Rushing is usually an indication that the horse is trying to avoid the exercise. The rider should slow the pace and progress quietly.

Problem: The horse has a tendency to slow the pace.

Solution: The horse should not be allowed to reduce or increase the pace or to change the gait. The rider must always have the horse in front of the legs so that the horse responds immediately to changes and transitions as demanded by the rider. The basic exercises provided in *Divide and Conquer Book 1* should be reviewed and practiced.

Nota Bene

Leg Yielding. The leg yielding exercise is mentioned in a note because it does not qualify as a true lateral movement. Although the horse is crossing his front and back legs while moving in a sideways direction, the horse's spine is not BENT.

Leg yielding seems to emanate from an incorrect interpretation of the French term, *cession à la jambe,* which, when translated means cession to the leg. In cession to the leg, the horse bends his spine; the exercise is a pedagogic aid to teach horses and riders to travel sideways. At the superior level, when the horse is displacing himself sideways, the horse will be withdrawing his ribs, raising his back, and lifting the base of his neck to become more rounded and balanced. Leg yielding produces nothing except the crossing of the legs.

Masters discovered that leg yielding provides riders with an exercise to properly apply and coordinate their lateral aids, using a right indirect rein and right leg behind the girth or vice versa. In the leg yielding exercise, however, the horse commonly makes the error of an awkward and uncomfortable "S" spinal position in which his head is turned toward one side while his body remains straight and his haunches deviate toward the opposite side. Overzealous practice often creates more problems than it provides solutions and can result in a horse's lameness. As my Veterinarian friend has always said, "Ninety percent of a horse's lameness is generally the result of unorthodox equitation."

In the early 1900s, and still today, the fad of leg yielding as an exercise has been introduced and dropped from dressage tests. Active debate may continue regarding the usefulness of the leg yielding exercise.

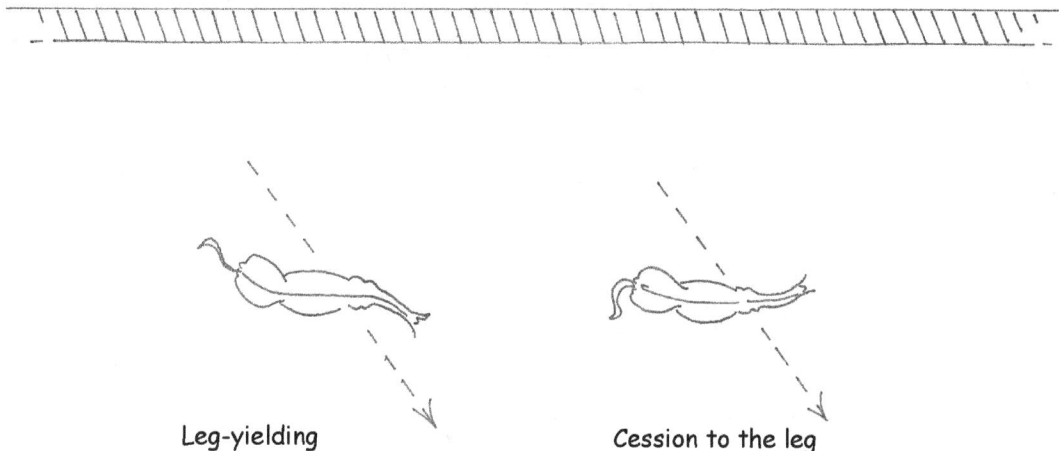

Leg-yielding   Cession to the leg

Figure 34 - Leg yielding compared to cession to the leg

Pirouette and Counter-Pirouette

The pirouettes and counter-pirouettes are very tight circles on four tracks. The correct executions of the pirouettes, especially around the haunches, are difficult and must be studied at an advanced stage of the horse's training. Pirouettes and counter-pirouettes are well-known to induce remarkable mobility.

Pirouette

A pirouette is a rotation of the horse's shoulders around the haunches. The pirouette can be performed at a standstill step-by-step, at the walk, trot, or canter. When the pirouette is performed at standstill the movement is called a turn around the haunches. When initiated from motion, the turn is known as a pirouette.

Pirouettes are basically tight voltes on four tracks. Their correct execution is difficult and should be demanded at an advance stage of training.

Goals of the Pirouette

1. To further develop the horse's agility in the shoulders and anterior limbs.

2. To enable the horse to shift his weight onto the posteriors, thereby lightening the horse's forehand.

3. To shorten and inflate the horse's loin muscles, flex the pelvic muscles, and lower the haunches.

Advantages and Inconveniences of Pirouettes

While a pirouette can accomplish developing lightness in the horse's forehand, it reduces the activity of the posteriors due to the increased weight the horse must carry on the haunches.

Rider's Aids for a Pirouette (The rider's aids are provided for a pirouette to the right; the opposite aids are used in a pirouette to the left.)

Hands: The rider's right hand acts as a direct rein to lead the horse to the right. The rider's left hand acts as a light indirect rein of opposition in front of the withers to stimulate the horse's left shoulder toward the right.

Legs: The rider's right leg acts at the girth to bend the horse's spine and maintain the impulsion. The rider's left leg acts behind the girth to prevent the haunches from deviating to the outside.

Seat: The rider should rotate the hips toward the direction of movement (the left hip is more forward), while slightly increasing the weight on the right seat bone and right stirrup.

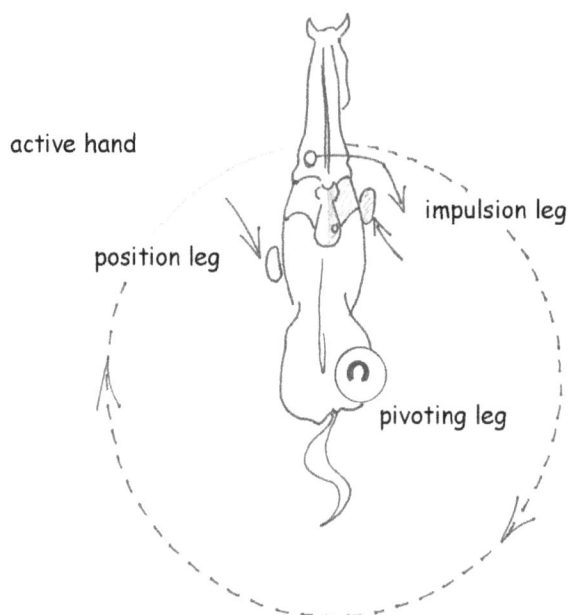

active hand

position leg

impulsion leg

pivoting leg

Figure 35 - Aids for the pirouette

Nota Bene

When the horse is first learning the pirouette, the rider should begin from a shoulder-in position and change to position the horse in a counter bend. When the horse is turning to the right, his nose will be turned to the left. Despite this early sacrifice of position, the horse will realize much benefit. It is important not to rush or force the horse and only move to the next phase when the horse shows sufficient progress. As soon as the horse shows capability to better perform this rotation around the haunches, the rider should thereafter make certain that the horse is looking in the direction of the motion. When training at the advanced level, rider should subtly and imperceptibly change the horse's bend at the poll every two or three strides to make certain that the horse does not become locked at the poll.

The rider should always first teach the horse to rotate around the haunches from a standing (halt) position and proceed very slowly one step at a time. Begin with quarter (90 degrees) and half turns (180 degrees) before demanding full (360 degree) pirouette. As the horse turns, the rider must make certain that the horse pivots around the inside hind leg on the direction of the turn, i.e. for a pirouette to the right, the horse should pivot around the right posterior when turning left, the horse should pivot around the left hind leg. Pivoting around the wrong hind leg creates a retrograde movement and results in blocking the horse's posteriors. The rider should maintain activity to prevent the horse from planting his hind leg on the ground but actually make certain that the standing leg continues to step up and down and maintain the foot sequences of the determined gait.

Exercises to Develop the Pirouette

1. Follow the pattern of an octagon and move the shoulder one step at each segment.

2. Follow the pattern of a hexagon and move the shoulder one step at each segment.

3. Follow the pattern of a square and move the horse's shoulders two steps at each corner.

4. Follow the pattern of a triangle and move the shoulder three steps at each corner.

5. Follow the pattern of a half-circle (180 degrees).

6. Travel in a counter-shoulder-in on a 10-meter circle.

7. Travel with the haunches toward the inside on a 10-meter circle.

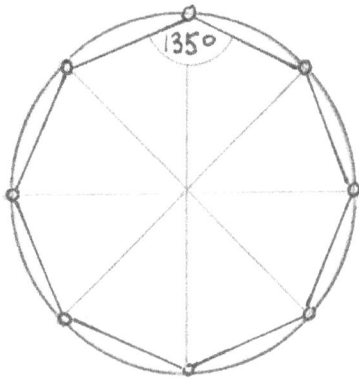

Octagonal

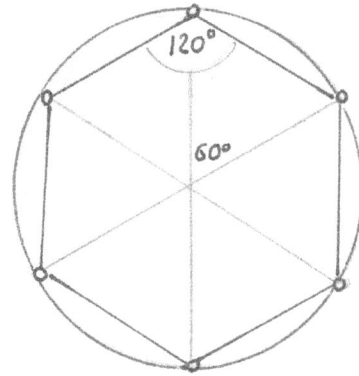

Hexagonal

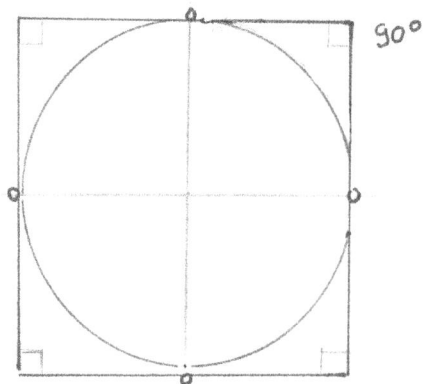

Square

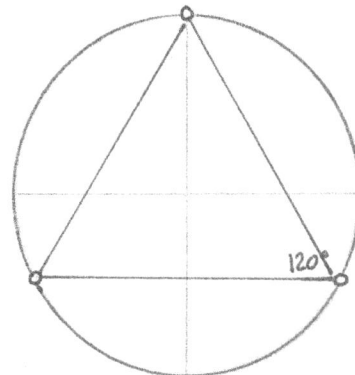

Triangle

Figure 36 - Octagon, Hexagon, Square, Triangle

Troubleshooting

Problem: The horse cannot or does not want to displace his shoulders to the right or left.

Solution: The rider must review and practice all exercises described in *Divide and Conquer Book 1*, which include leading the shoulders, pushing the shoulders, spiraling in and out of circles and zigzagging. With the same hand, alternating the use of direct and indirect rein aids will remedy the problem. In *Divide and Conquer Book 1*, I explain zigzagging. For example, the rider should lead the horse to the left with the left direct rein and ask the horse to veer to the right with the left indirect rein.

Problem: The horse turns too widely.

Solution: Turning too widely is an indication that the horse lacks suppleness. The horse needs more time and practice. Daily sessions will progressively teach the horse to make tighter turns. The rider should remember that after moving the shoulder she should perform the complementary exercise by rotating the haunches around the shoulders. The rider should reinforce the aids to better help the horse without pulling the horse.

Problem: The horse turns too slowly.

Solution: The lack of agility will cause the horse to turn slower. The rider should practice the half-turn following a much wider pattern. Each time the horse slows the pace, the rider should leave the exercise and send the horse forward on a tangent line. With practice and in time, the horse will develop the ability to turn tighter and maintain an even tempo.

Nota Bene

When performing the pirouette at the trot, the rider should follow the same exercises that were performed at the walk but in a slightly wider pattern so that the horse will be able to pivot on both hind legs with animation.

The pirouettes at the trot and at the canter belong to the high school movements because they require a horse to possess great suppleness over the entire body. He must be well-acquainted with all lateral exercises. The pirouettes produce much mobility but are generally more stressful on the hocks of young mares than young male horses that do not possess the same resistance. In the major riding schools of Europe, stallions and geldings are preferred since male horses genetically possess inherently greater strength in their hind legs. These are the stallions chosen for breeding. Although mares can perform the same movements, they assume greater risk in damaging their hind joints and care should be taken to not over-task a mare.

Pirouette at the Canter

A high degree of collection is demanded to properly perform a pirouette at the canter.

Teaching the Horse the Right Canter Pirouette

1. Collect the canter and maintain the horse's straightness. The horse should be round, light and in balance.

2. Ride each stride of the canter in cadence, without rushing, so that the horse continues to propel himself and lower his haunches.

3. The rider must maintain a proper straight posture yet look toward the destination. i.e. look to the left for the left pirouette and vice versa. The direct rein leads the horse into the pirouette. To create a better pirouette:

    • Look in the direction of the pirouette, i.e. for a right pirouette, the rider should be looking right.

    • The rider should slightly rotate her hips to the inside with her outside hip moving forward.

    • The rider will displace both hands slightly toward the inside of the turn using a light inside direct rein, accompanied alternately with an outside indirect rein. Both reins remain soft.

    • The rider's inside leg acts at the girth to maintain the activity of the inside posterior. She firmly resists with her outside leg behind the girth to contain any potential displacement of the haunches toward the outside and to perform a better turn.

4. While pirouetting around the inside posterior, the rider should sustain and maintain each canter stride without interrupting the horse's balance. The rider should manifest the impression of riding a very tight half-pass so that the

horse will not rush the movement, lose his balance and, as a consequence, fall inward and decompose the canter pirouette into 4 or 5 strides instead of the preferred 6 or 8 strides.

Figure 37 - Canter pirouette

Plate 2: Canter pirouette executed by a Louis XIV rider. Painting by François
Lemaire de Ruffieu

64

Exercises to Aid in Preparation for the Canter Pirouette

Before attempting the following exercises at the canter, the rider should practice and perfect the displacement of the horse's shoulder by riding zigzags alternating the two indirect reins without losing the quality of the canter.

Phase One. Prerequisite for a Pirouette at the Canter

1. Ride a canter half-pass and gradually alternate the speed.

2. Perfect the transitions of walk—canter—walk—canter.

3. Beginning on a wide circle and progressively reduce the diameter to a volte, canter in the shoulder-in and haunches-in.

When the horse is able, gradually reduce the diameter of the circle while maintaining the canter.

4. On a wide circle and then on a volte, practice the transitions: canter—walk—rein-back—walk—canter followed by canter—halt—rein-back—canter.

5. On a straight line perform a light shoulder-in followed by canter—halt—rein-back—canter transitions.

6. In a light shoulder-in (shoulder-fore), the rider follows the pattern of an octagon by pushing the horse's shoulders inside at the end of each segment.

7. Following the pattern of a hexagon, the horse will be asked to pivot one step.

8. Following the pattern of a square, the horse will be asked to pivot two steps.

9. Following the pattern of a triangle, the horse will be asked to pivot three steps.

All of the patterns should be large at the beginning of the practice. Over time, the patterns should become tighter.

Phase Two

1. The rider performs a pirouette at the walk but at a previously decided point, the rider demands a canter departure, maintains the canter for ONE stride only on the pirouette and immediately leaves the pattern by moving straight forward to prevent the horse from falling inside the turn, then returns to the walk and rewards the horse.

2. While performing a pirouette at the walk, at a previously decided point, the rider demands a canter departure and maintains the horse at the canter for TWO strides before leaving the pattern.

3. While performing a pirouette at the walk the rider demands THREE canter strides and proceeds in the above-stated manner.

4. The rider continues this progression, gradually increasing the number of canter strides.

Phase Three

The rider will proceed in the same manner as in Phase Two but in this phase, the rider will maintain the horse in a constant small pirouette.

1. From a pirouette at a walk, the rider asks for ONE canter stride and walks again in the pirouette.

2. From a pirouette at the walk, the rider asks for TWO consecutive strides at the canter and returns to the pirouette at the walk.

3. From a pirouette at the walk, the rider asks for THREE consecutive canter strides and returns to the pirouette at the walk, gradually increasing the number of canter strides to between six to eight canter strides.

After completing these three phases of work, on an inside track about 6 meters from the wall of the arena, the rider should begin at the counter-canter and ask for a half-pirouette turning toward the outside, i.e. the wall, which is a wonderful pedagogic aid. This exercise will invite the horse to turn and compel the rider to ride every stride with undivided attention. As the horse develops the ability to easily turn toward the wall, the rider should demand the same outside pirouette but move progressively closer to the wall. When the horse shows distinct signs of ease, the wall will no longer be necessary.

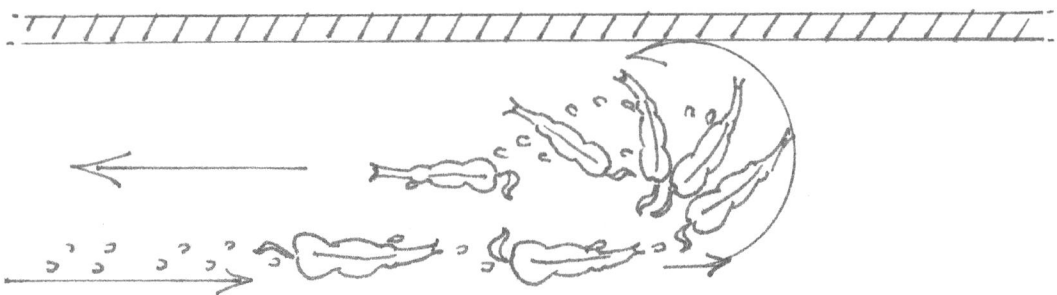

Figure 38 - Canter pirouette turning toward the wall

After collecting the canter for two or three strides, the rider can randomly practice quarter, half, and full pirouettes. The rider should always remember that pirouettes are difficult exercises for the horse and should not abuse the good will of the animal. If difficulties occur, the rider should go back and review the previous exercises.

Troubleshooting

Problem: The horse falls toward the inside.

Solution: Practice Step one of Phase Two of the above exercises to teach the horse to better maintain his balance.

Problem: The horse breaks from the canter after two or three strides.

Solution: The breaking of the gait indicates a lack of impulsion. The rider should support the canter with her inside leg at the girth. Practicing lengthening and shortening of the canter will aid in developing the horse's impulsion.

Problem: The horse has difficulty turning.

Solution: If the horse shows difficulties in turning, the rider should practice the pirouette at the walk and trot for a longer period of time or work in hand.

Figure 39 - Work in hand

The beauty of the canter pirouette is in the slow cadence of the canter and the amplification of the rotation of the shoulders around the haunches. To best perform a canter pirouette, the horse will lower his haunches and add an extra beat to the three-beat canter. For a left pirouette, the horse will move his right posterior followed by the left posterior, then the right anterior, and the left forefoot last. The time of suspension is not perceptible. Although some horses may complete the pirouette in six to eight steps, the fewer number of steps indicates a higher degree of collection while a greater number of steps can indicate balance problems.

Counter Pirouette

A counter pirouette is a rotation of the horse's haunches around the shoulders. It can be performed on a quarter circle, half-circle or full circle. When it is performed from the halt the movement is known as a turn around the shoulders. When it is performed in motion, it is known as a counter pirouette. The counter pirouette is generally performed at the walk or trot. When it is performed at the canter, the horse may tend to cross-canter, i.e. canter on the right lead with his anteriors while simultaneously cantering on the left lead with his posteriors or vice versa.

Figure 40 - Moving the haunches

Goals for the Counter Pirouette

1. To develop the suppleness of the horse's haunches and the agility of the horse's posteriors.

2. To stretch and flex the muscles in the loins.

3. To incite the horse to mobilize his mouth, flex at the poll (between Atlas and Axis vertebrae), and to better come onto the bit.

4. To lower or raise the poll as a function of the position of the neck, i.e. to lower the poll, the horse's neck should be bent on the same side as the acting leg; to raise the poll, the head and neck should be absolutely straight.

Advantages and Inconveniences of the Counter Pirouette

The counter pirouette can be used to revivify the activity of the posteriors. When the horse performs a true pirouette, the benefit is to free the shoulders by shifting the center of gravity toward the haunches. However, the risk is a reduction in the activity of the horse's posteriors due to the shifting of weight onto the haunches. The counter-pirouette will recreate the activity of the posteriors.

Rider's Aids for a Counter Pirouette when tracking to the right

(Opposite aids are used when tracking left.)

Hands: The rider's right hand acts with an indirect rein to maintain the horse's nose to the right and to weight the left shoulder. The rider's left hand yields and then regulates the action of the right hand.

Legs: The rider's right leg acts at the girth to maintain the activity and the right bend. The rider's left leg acts behind the girth to stimulate the horse's haunches to the right.

Seat: The rider's should shift the weight onto the right seat bone.

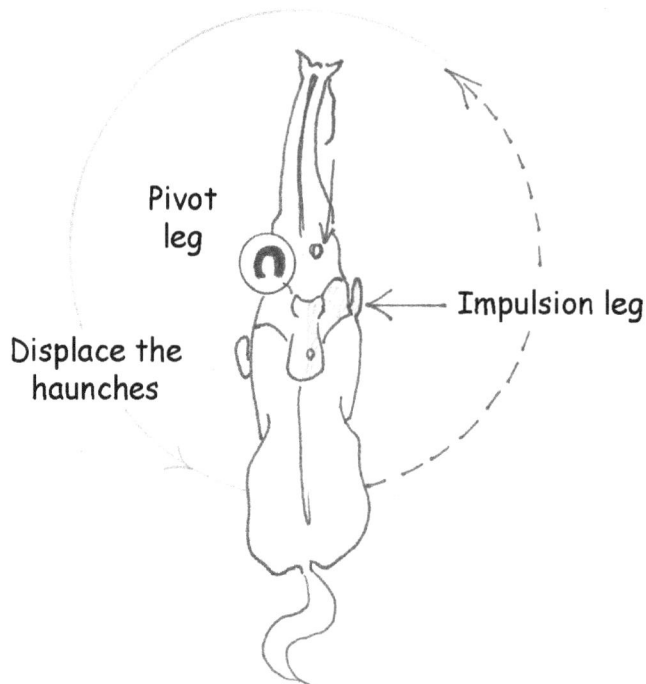

Figure 41 - Aids to move the haunches

Preparation for Performing a Counter Pirouette

1. The rider executes a right shoulder-in on an 8-10 meter circle.

2. The rider maintains the same aids for the shoulder-in as she progressively reduces the size of the circle by spiraling inward.

3. As the rider reaches the center of the circle she should push the horse's haunches around the outside anterior limb in such a way that this anterior will move up and down to fall back in the same hoof print while the horse's haunches rotate around the forehand.

Counter-pirouettes should first be taught to the horse from a halt, quietly, one step at a time. The rider should progress to a slow walk before demanding the counter pirouette, with increased activity for quarter turns and half turns before demanding a full counter pirouette. As the horse pivots around his shoulders, the rider must make certain that the horse pivots on the right anterior, rotating the haunches around the outside anterior (for a turn from right to left). The pivoting leg will be animated as opposed to being planted on the ground and will move up and down to maintain the order of steps in the gait. Allowing the horse to pivot around the wrong anterior will diminish the training and may cause the horse to acquire defenses.

Exercises to Develop and Improve the Counter Pirouette

1. Following the pattern of a square, the rider halts at each corner and stimulates the haunches toward the outside around the shoulders for a total of two steps. The same exercise is repeated at each of the four corners. When the horse shows no resistances and easily displaces his haunches, the same exercise can be performed at a slow walk, a faster walk, and finally at the trot.

2. Following the pattern of a triangle, the rider performs the same exercise as stated above, moving the haunches toward the outside at each point of the triangle.

3. The rider follows the pattern of a half-circle and at points 180 degrees apart, pivots two steps.

4. After progressing conscientiously through these exercises, the rider should be able to perform a full counter-pirouette (360 degree turn).

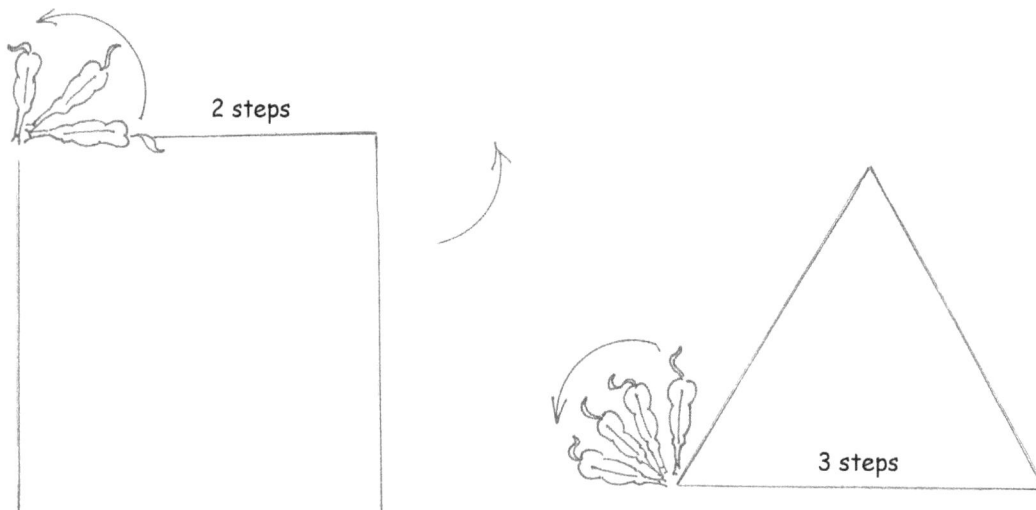

Figure 42 - Pushing the haunches; square; triangle

Troubleshooting

Problem: The horse steps backward.

Solution: The horse is pivoting around the wrong anterior or the rider is pulling on the reins to restrain the horse from trying to escape the exercise by moving forward. The rider must be very light with the reins and make certain that the horse is pivoting around the outside anterior. (For a turn from right to left, the horse will pivot on the right foreleg; the left foreleg is the pivoting leg when turning from left to right.)

Problem: The horse steps forward but does not turn.

Solution: The horse is trying to avoid the exercise. To solve the problem the rider should resist with his/her back without pulling on the reins. If the horse does not respond well to the rider's aids, the rider should review all transitions with special emphasis on the downward transitions.

Problem: The horse slows the pace.

Solution: Failure to maintain the pace is indicative of the horse's difficulty in displacing his haunches. Review the exercises in the order described. Beginning again from the halt will remedy the problem.

Problem: The horse has difficulty moving his haunches from a standing position.

Solution: The rider should reteach the horse to displace his haunches in hand from the ground. Each day, before mounting the horse, the rider should spend a few minutes on the ground and ask the horse to move his haunches.

A great gymnastic is to alternate a half-pirouette followed immediately by a half counter pirouette several times one after the other. Well-executed, these two exercises will prove the lightness of the horse's forehand, suppleness of the horses' shoulders, strength of his loins and the submission of the haunches.

At any time, if the horse displays weakness in the activity, the rider should leave the exercise and send the horse energetically forward on a straight line before recommencing the exercise.

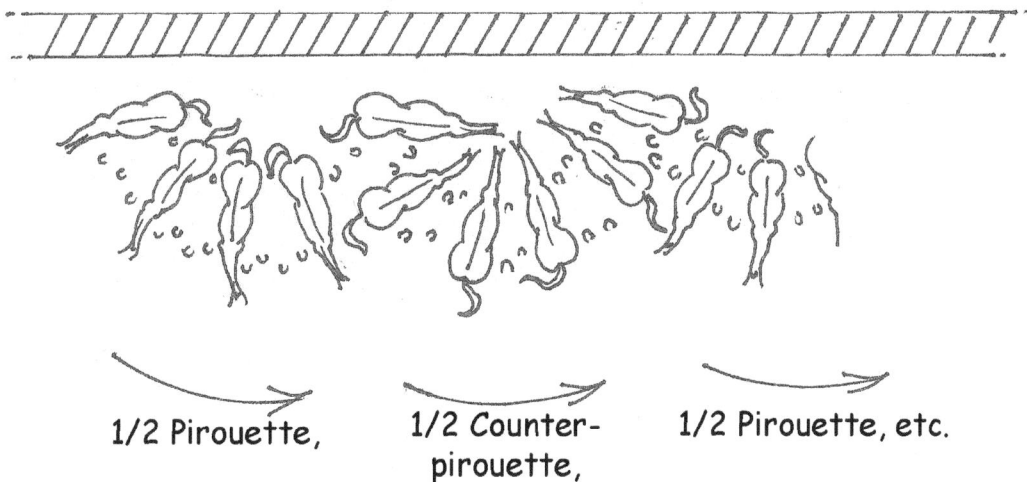

1/2 Pirouette,   1/2 Counter-pirouette,   1/2 Pirouette, etc.

Figure 43 - Half-pirouette, counter pirouette

Nota Bene

When the rider performs a counter pirouette at the walk and maintains the horse's nose and neck bent on the same side as the rider's leg acting behind the girth, the horse will have the tendency to lower his front end. This physical reaction may help the rider to teach the horse to stretch downward long and low or extension d'encolure.

When the rider performs a counter pirouette at the walk but maintains the head and neck absolutely straight, the horse will have a tendency to raise his neck and head. This physical reaction may help the rider to correct a horse that has a tendency to maintain his head behind the vertical and is a very useful method to correct the deep and low attitude too often encountered that indicates inherent weakness or a false means of domination and ultimately prevents the horse from performing to the best of his abilities.

CHAPTER FOUR

Flying Changes of Lead

A flying change of lead is a canter departure to the opposite lead when the horse is already at the canter. For example, when the horse is cantering on the right lead, the horse performs a change of lead during the suspension phase to depart and change to the left lead or vice versa.

While horses can walk and trot in only one manner, horses can canter in two different ways: on the right lead or on the left lead. An isolated flying change of lead consists of changing from one canter lead to the other while still maintaining the canter.

As the horse advances in his education, the horse should be able to perform several consecutive changes in a row and gradually change leads at closer intervals, i.e, every five, four, three, and two strides. When a horse has been properly trained, the horse should be able to change canter leads at every stride as required at the Grand Prix dressage level. While most horses should be able to change leads at least every two strides, only horses carefully trained and sufficiently agile will be able to properly change leads at every stride.

Demanding a Flying Change of Lead

The commands for a flying change of lead are provided when the horse is already at the canter on the right lead and changing to the left lead.

While maintaining an even tempo on the right lead canter, the rider should make certain that the horse is balanced and straight before simultaneously reversing her canter aids by moving her left leg forward near the girth and her right leg slightly behind the girth, and then act with both legs to demand the change. The horse's head should remain straight.

The essentials of obtaining a flying change of lead are as follows:

1. The *sine qua non* conditions to obtain a flying change of lead are:

- a calm, steady active canter.

- the horse remains straight and in perfect balance.

2. At a previously chosen place, the rider applies a brief half-parade (see definition in the index) on the side of the original lead to warn the horse and lighten his forehand and then quietly rides two or three strides with a little more determination without changing speed before demanding the actual change of lead to the left.

- Position must always precede the action. To ask for the left lead canter change, the rider simultaneously places her left leg closer to the girth and her right leg slightly behind the girth and then acts with both legs simultaneously as if she wanted to shift the horse into a half-pass to the left.

Displacing the haunches to the left causes the horse to bring the left hock forward and recreate the horse's natural position when he is cantering on the left lead. In other words, the horse merely traverses himself to the left for the left lead and vice versa for the right lead canter to recreate his natural tendency to canter slightly sideways.

- The rider must sit straight yet invisibly lean her upper body toward the new lead. The rider's change of upper body position must remain absolutely discrete. Excess rider movement is not only disgraceful, but it obfuscates the aids and results in the loss of flying changes' elegance.

- It is IMPORTANT that the rider must look in the direction of the motion at eye level.

- The contact of the reins with the horse's mouth should be light and equal on both sides. The horse's head should remain straight.

- Prompt and precise use of the aids is essential. After the change of lead has been demanded, the rider may have to wait until the change has occurred. The rider must be patient because the horse is the one actually executing the change.

- Following the change of lead, the rider should maintain the horse's straightness and contain the gait in the event that the horse may accelerate the pace.

- It is necessary to emphasize that it is not the perfection of change but it is the efficacy that the rider should first seek while maintaining impulsion.

- In the future the horse will learn to switch canter leads without displacing his haunches to the side. The closer the changes are demanded, true straightness will be of greater importance.

Rider's Mistakes due to Inexperience

- Rushing the horse to change the lead. The novice rider should take her time to place her aids and then ask for the change.
- Becoming tense and holding her breath. Breathing quietly will enhance relaxation.
- Raising her hands instead of keeping them low.
- Leaving the seat of the saddle instead of sitting deeply.
- Failure to look where she is going and lowering her eyes.

Horse's Mistakes

- Changing speeds before or after the change.
- Failure to remain calm and steady.
- Changing leads in front without changing leads behind.
- Changes lead before being asked.

Because the canter is composed of four phases, Riding Masters have maintained different theories on timing of when the demand is best given to maintain the calm, steadiness, and straightness in a well-balanced horse. Suggestions comprise the following:

- The demand should be applied from right to left lead when the horse's left diagonal biped is on the ground, i.e. between the second phase (the outside diagonal biped is leading) and third phase (the inside anterior is leading) of the canter.
- The demand should be applied when the horse's front end is descending (during the third phase of the canter).
- The demand should be applied when the horse is in the suspension phase of the canter, i.e. between the third and fourth sequence of the canter.

- The general consensus is that for the average rider, the best time to demand a flying change is when the horse's diagonal biped is on the ground, i.e. during the second phase of the canter.

- (For the right lead canter, the horse's left diagonal biped will be on the ground.) At this precise moment, the rider should ask for the left lead because the horse's right posterior is about to propel the horse forward.

Nota Bene

Although opinions vary from one Master to another, all are correct because an absolute answer does not exist in the case of the flying change. Beyond the art of dressage and the science of the horse's motion, tact and quickness of the rider's aids are of key importance to precision and promptness in the horse's response. It is for each rider to study and discover what is best. Practice, observation, and reflection will aid in the rider's development.

- *A novice rider will realize the change of lead after it has been accomplished.*

- *An advanced rider will feel the change as it occurs.*

- *A confirmed rider will anticipate and sense how and when to prepare the demand properly.*

The rider should apply her aids with maximum discretion, which is a function of tact, concentration, and sensation. The horse that is well-trained will require only the most discreet aids. The horse must be absolutely obedient to the rider's slightest demand. Nevertheless, while learning the flying change, the rider should not seek perfection but efficacy. The rider should neither push nor rush the demand for the change of lead but wait until it occurs. The horse must learn not to anticipate or precipitate the changes. The rider must remember, however, that even when the horse is solicited to make the change, if the flying change is not instantaneous, the rider must wait as it is the horse that must accomplish the change in lead.

Prerequisites for Teaching the Horse the Flying Change

For the Horse

Proper preparation in obtaining good canter departures will avoid defective flying changes. Before teaching a horse to change leads, the rider must have sufficient practice and mastery of skill in the precision of aids, i.e. the coordination of the horse, rider, and equestrian tact.

The horse should be able to strike into the canter from the walk, halt, and rein-back without hesitation equally well on both leads. The rider should teach the horse to perfectly and instantaneously respond to the slightest aids. The horse must become very receptive to the rider's most discreet solicitation. The horse must not accelerate the pace when the rider applies her leg at the girth or behind it.

The horse should easily be able to maintain the counter-canter in both directions on a straight line as well as on circles.

The horse should be able to perform all rudimentary elements of the half-pass at the canter in both directions.

For the Rider

The rider should be able to effortlessly maintain the horse's straightness and balance in a steady canter. Each horse is different, and the rider should determine what natural pace is best for each particular horse she is riding. The canter should have a steady tempo.

The rider must be able to accelerate or slow the pace at any time without any effort.

The rider must be able to turn the horse's nose to either side *(pli)* without interfering with the gait or the horse's balance at the canter and the counter-canter. The mastery of this skill is proof that the horse does not resist in his neck.

The horse must always remain perpendicular to the ground and not lean toward the inside on a circle of any diameter. To accomplish this goal, the rider must be able to slightly bend both extremities of the horse simultaneously as in combining a shoulder-in with a haunches-in, i.e., the idea of a half-pass staying on track without drifting.

The rider must be able to spiral in and out within a circumference.

Nota Bene

The rider must avoid asking for the canter departure from the trot because the horse will generate the lead from his anteriors. Rider should remember that a canter departure solicited from the walk will compel the horse to strike off from his posteriors. In a flying change the horse should generate the lead change from his hind legs.

Troubleshooting

Problem: The horse does not change leads.

Solution: If a horse does not change leads, it is an indication that the horse has not yet acquired the necessary receptiveness to the aids and is not yet ready to perform the changes. Practice and study of the upward and downward transitions will correct the problem. Confirming the canter departures on both leads will prevent the lack of response when the rider solicits the flying change.

It is important that the rider remember that a horse may take some time before the demand for a flying change is clearly understood. The horse may hesitate before he becomes comfortable with associating a change of lead with a demand. The rider must be patient.

Problem: The horse initiates the change of lead with his anteriors.

Solution: This mistake should be an indication to the rider that preparation is lacking. Impulsion, balance and straightness must be reviewed and improved. When the rider is demanding a flying change, the rider may apply the whip on the horse's thigh on the same side as the rider's leg behind the girth, i.e. for a change from the right to left, the whip should be applied on the horse's right thigh and vice versa for a change from left to right, but the aid of the whip should not be relied upon without the proper time and effort put forth in preparation. Changes in lead should be demanded on a circle with a cession to the legs from the counter-canter to the inside lead.

Problem: The horse changes lead with the posteriors before the anteriors have changed leads.

Solution: This delay is not exactly a problem. It simply means that the horse is properly changing leads with his hind legs without changing leads with his front legs. A little more experience and practice with the flying changes will compel the horse to correct this situation by himself. Actually, this problem might be most fortunate as the horse will never change leads late in his posteriors.

Problem: The horse increased the canter speed in anticipation of the change of lead.

Solution: Increasing the speed is a sign of evasion. Speed is not a criterion of impulsion. The horse must learn to maintain the same pace when the rider is soliciting a flying change. The canter should be active within the same pace. Reviewing upward and downward transitions within the same gait will remedy the problem. The rider should postpone the changes for a period of time until the horse has regained total calmness.

Problem: The horse changes lead in one direction but not the other.

Solution: If, for example, it is easier for the horse to change canter leads from right to left versus from left to right, it usually means that the canter departures on the right lead are not as correct as the left lead. Unless something is physically wrong with the horse, the rider should review and perfect the canter departures toward the right lead. It would be the opposite if the horse has difficulties change lead in the opposite direction.

Problem: The horse has a tendency to buck as the change occurs.

Solution: Until the horse has learned the changes of lead properly, he may buck a little (or more) to bend his spine to accomplish the change of lead in his posteriors. The problem indicates a lack of balance. The rider should not sit heavily but even lighten her seat in the saddle. Bucking can also indicate that the pace of the canter was either too slow or too fast and that the horse cannot bend his spine properly. The rider should increase or decrease the pace, making certain that the horse is not running but is engaged.

Nota Bene

When the horse is learning flying changes, it is important that the rider not demand too many changes during the early sessions. The rider should never force the horse to the changes but ask and allow the change.

81

In other words, the rider should place the aids, demand the action with her legs, and wait for the horse to change leads. Practicing a few lead changes every other session should be sufficient until the horse has truly understood and accepted the demand and is able to change leads properly. The rider should always reward the horse afterwards and keep in mind that horses, like people, can become tired after a long or too intense work-study. The rider should always remember that a horse will do well only what the horse likes to do. The rider should always present the work-study in such a way that the horse enjoys the work.

Initiating Study of the Flying Change

Although there is no precise time when the study of the flying changes should begin, it is always a good idea to wait until the horse is sufficient in his education, both mentally and physically. The rider should begin teaching the flying changes only when the horse is steady in the canter and counter-canter, well-balanced and straight in both directions. The horse should be able to maintain a horizontal balance, meaning that the horse's weight is equally distributed without the horse shifting more weight to either his forehand or on his haunches. When the rider practices the simplest changes of lead, i.e. changes of lead through the walk or the halt, the horse may, at some time, steal a flying change. Should this happen more than once, the horse is clearly telling the rider that it may be time to advance to the next level, i.e. the flying changes.

To begin the study, the rider should demand a right lead canter departure from the walk and maintain the canter for only a few strides and directly return to the walk. Then, from the walk, the rider should ask for a left lead canter departure and maintain the canter for a few strides and return to the walk. The rider should continue alternating the different canter departures between the walk. Gradually the rider should reduce the number of walking strides between the canter departures until the horse is able to easily walk only one stride between each canter departure.

To avoid routine and anticipation, the rider should vary the canter departures between the walking strides. Sometimes the rider might request the same canter departure between walking strides and surprise the horse by asking for the alternate departure lead, i.e., two departures to the right lead, one departure to the left lead, three to the right, two to the left, one to the right, etc...

When the horse can execute these transitions well at close intervals, he will be ready to try the flying changes. If the preparatory work-study was well-accomplished, the horse should easily be able to change leads. In the beginning, the rider may be required to act firmer in her leg aids, but the rider should never hurry the horse. After the rider asks for the change of leads, the rider should wait until it occurs and not precipitate the action. Some horses may require more time to understand what is being expected of him. Some horses can learn very quickly provided that the rider explains what is being asked over a long period of time. Sometimes, rest and reflection provide the desired results. For some horses, the flying change might be better taught on a straight line versus circles as circles may incite the horse to steal the change from loss of balance.

Classical Methods of Teaching the Flying Changes

In the progression of the dressage, the rider should demand the flying changes as follows:

- on a circle from the counter-canter to the inside lead
- on a straight line from the counter-canter to the inside lead
- on a straight line from the inside lead to the counter-canter
- on a circle from the inside lead to the counter-canter.

Other *manège* figures used to teach the flying changes:

- half-voltes and the half-volte in reverse
- serpentines
- counter-changes
- figure eights (two tangent circles)

Proven Methods to Teach the Flying Change

Method One:

Before beginning to follow the pattern of a large circle, the rider should decide where to ask for a flying change. For example, in a dressage arena, the rider, on a twenty-meter circle in the center of the arena between letters E and B, may decide that the flying change will be demanded at letter B.

Phase 1. From a standing position at B, the rider walks two or three strides and strikes off into the canter on the inside lead and continues to canter the entire circumference and halt again shortly before reaching letter B. The rider should repeat the exercise several times with no change in the designated start and stopping point until the horse is performing well.

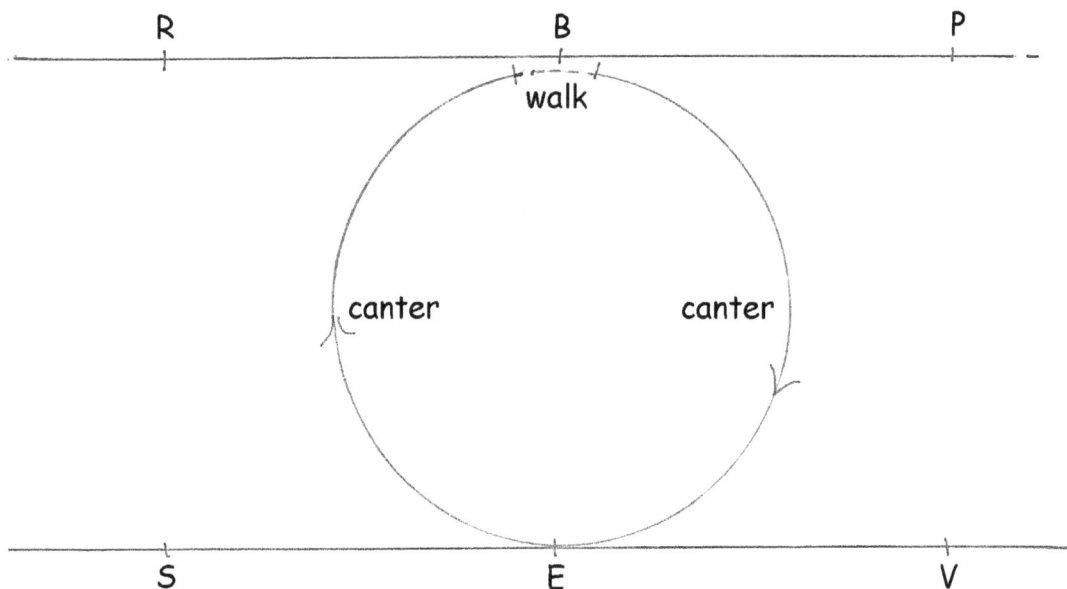

Figure 44 - Canter Depart at B

Phase 2. From the letter B, the rider begins again and maintains the counter-canter until stopping slightly before the letter B. This exercise should be repeated several times.

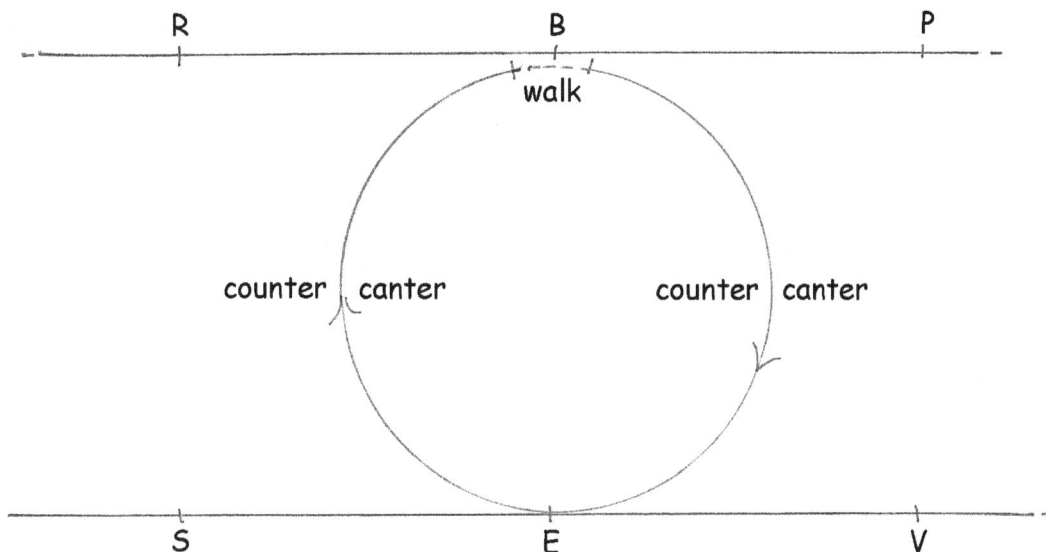

Figure 45 - At B ask for the inside lead departure

Phase 3. The rider should repeat Phase 1 and Phase 2 many times until she feels that her horse almost anticipates the canter at the letter B.

Phase 4. When the horse is comfortable cantering on both leads, ride the same circle at the counter-canter and at letter B, instead of walking, change the canter aids to demand the inside lead. By reflex or habit the horse should give a flying change.

Nota Bene

If the horse does not change leads, the rider should reestablish a tranquil walk and restudy Phases 1 and 2. The rider should never force the horse into the change of lead. If, after more work in performing the preceding exercises, the horse continues to show resistance and does not change leads, it is a sign that the horse is not yet ready to change leads at the canter.

Method Two:

Follow the pattern of a half-circle somewhat wider than a half-volte with a radius of 6 meters toward the inside of the arena followed by an oblique line of approximately 12 meters rejoining the track. The half-volte results in a change of direction.

Phase 1. The rider canters following the pattern of a half-circle toward the inside of the arena while maintaining the horse's haunches slightly toward the inside giving the idea of a travers.

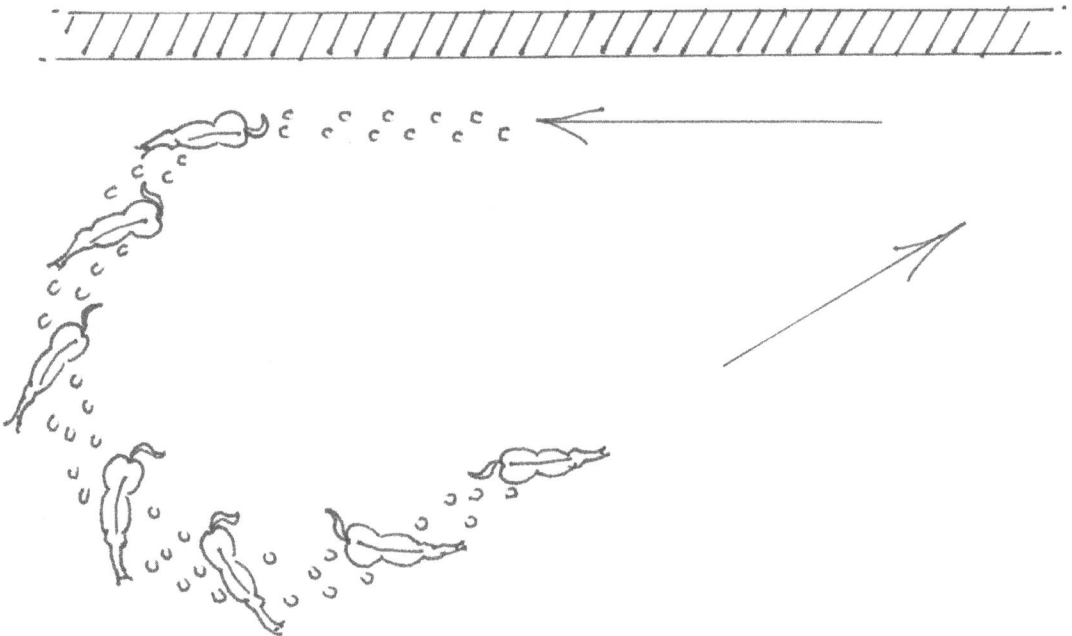

Figure 46 - Half-circle

Phase 2. At the end of the oblique line when the horse reaches the track, the rider should ask for two or three walking strides and then immediately demand the new inside lead. The rider should repeat this exercise several times, gradually reducing the number of walking strides from three to two to one.

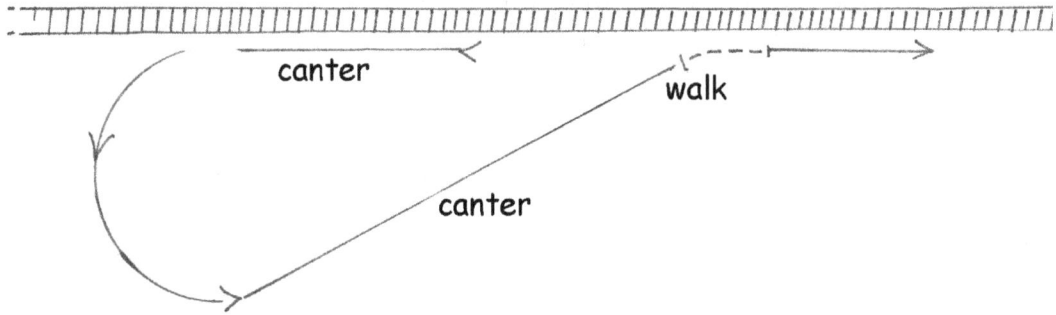

Figure 47 - Half-volte

Phase 3. Following the same pattern, at the conjunction point with the track, the rider will demand a change of lead. If the change is successful, the rider should walk her horse for a few minutes and reward him (rewarding the horse too soon breaks the horse's concentration).

Phase 4. The rider should repeat the same exercise only a few times in both directions. Over a period of time the horse will learn to perfect the flying changes. If the horse does not respond, it indicates that the horse does not understand what is being asked or that the horse is not quite ready to perform the task being demanded.

Method Three:

Phase 1. First at the walk, and then later at the trot, following the track on the short side of the arena, the rider should demand that the horse travel laterally with the haunches inside and nose outside (cession à la jambe or cession to the leg) on the short side. After the horse has passed the second corner of the short side and is entering the long side of the arena, the rider should change her leg aids to shift the horse's haunches to the outside and demand a counter-canter departure with both legs. After a few counter-canter strides, the rider should bring the horse back to the walk and reward him. Over a period of days, the rider should repeat this exercise many times until the horse strikes off into the counter-canter with perfect ease, almost on his own but still waiting for the rider's demand. Remember to practice this exercise both from the walk and from the trot in both directions.

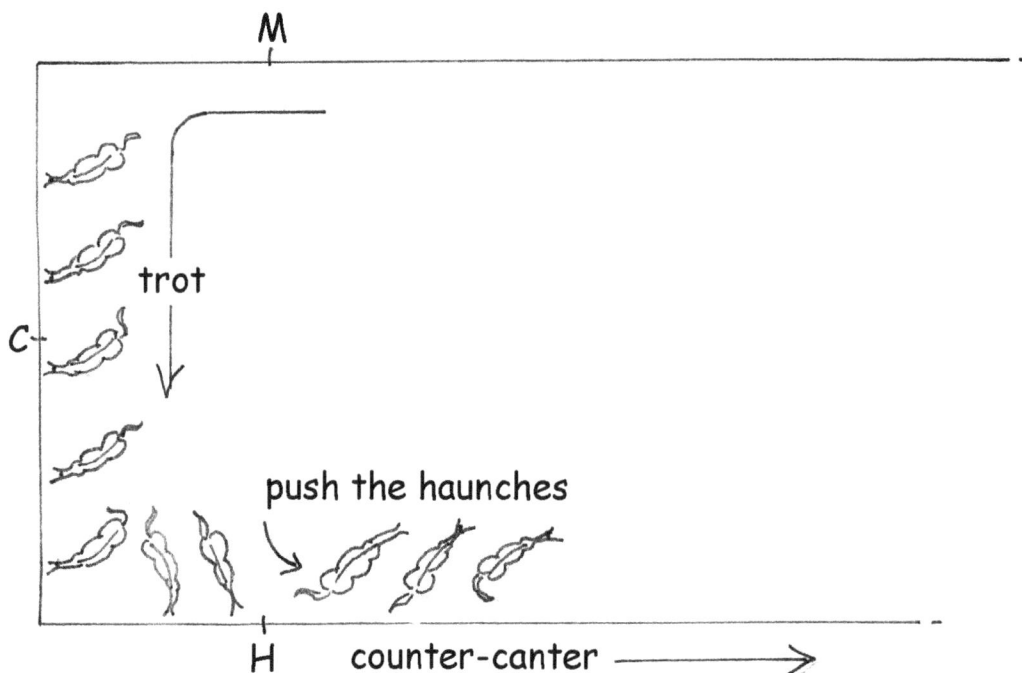

Figure 48 - Haunches into counter-canter

Phase 2. The rider should follow the same exercise but canter on the inside lead. As the rider reaches the short side of the arena, she should bring the horse's haunches on an inside track and maintain his nose to the outside. After the rider has passed the second corner of the short side of the arena, the rider should change her leg aids to shift the horse's haunches to the outside. As the horse was previously conditioned in Phase 1 to displace his haunches, the horse will change leads. The rider should then counter-canter a few strides before bringing the horse to the walk and rewarding him.

Note Bene

Practicing Phase 1 for several days and teaching the horse to begin the counter-canter at the same place is of key importance. If the horse does not change leads in practicing Phase 2, the rider should immediately demand the change one or two more times without changing the tempo but insist a little stronger with her leg back to displace the horse's haunches. If the horse still does not respond, it simply indicates that he is not yet ready, and the rider should practice Phase 1 for a few more days. If the horse changes lead, the rider can practice the same exercise every other day until the horse changes lead with ease almost by himself.

Method Four:

The rider follows the path of a counter-change of direction (riding two oblique lines in opposite directions).

Phase 1. Riding at the canter at the beginning of the long side of the arena, the rider follows the pattern of a counter-change, i.e. two opposite lines in different directions. On the first oblique line the rider places the horse into a half-pass toward the center line of the arena and asks the horse to walk and immediately to trot. Then follow the circumference of a 10-meter circle in the opposite direction of the half-pass, i.e. after a half-pass to the right the circle will be to the left (and vice versa following a half-pass to the left).

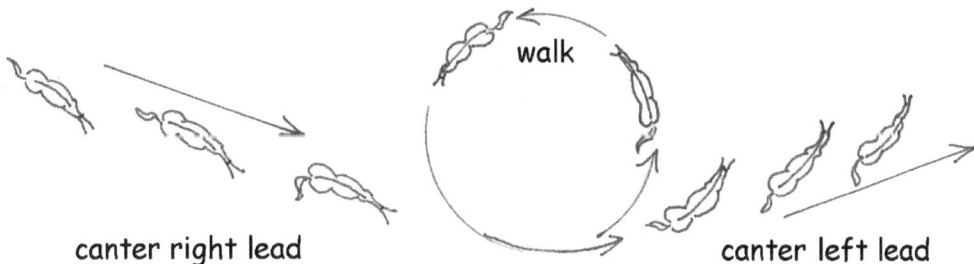

Figure 49 - Half-pass right, circle left, half-pass left

Phase 2. At the canter, the rider performs the half-pass on the oblique line. At the center line, the rider walks one or two strides, enters the circle and immediately demands the canter on the inside lead. She completes the circle and rides at the half-pass on the oblique line to return to the track. Before she reaches the end of the oblique line, the rider should return to the walk and reward her horse.

Phase 3. The rider canters at the half-pass on the first oblique line to reach the center line, walks one stride guiding the horse into the second oblique line and immediately asks for the alternate canter lead.

Phase 4. When the horse fully understands the exercise, the rider should proceed in the same manner as in Phase 3 except that she will NOT interrupt the canter as she reaches the center line. As the rider leads the horse into a half-pass to regain the track, the horse will switch leads toward the new direction. A horse that cannot perform the half-pass at the counter-canter will change leads.

Nota Bene

The circle between the two oblique lines is used to teach the rider to lead the horse in the new direction. Eliminating the circle from the exercise may result in the rider pushing the horse's haunches to excess and disturbing the change of lead.

Method Five:

Phase 1. Following the pattern of a figure eight of two, 10-15 meter circles, the rider maintains a shoulder-in at the trot. At the conjunction of the two circles, the rider maintains the same bend in the horse, transforming the shoulder-in to the haunches-out as the horse will now be bending towards the outside. At the end of the second half-circle, the rider changes the horse's body position from a haunches-out to a haunches-in. At the intersection of the two circles, the rider will change to a shoulder-out. At the end of the figure eight, the rider will walk and reward her horse.

When the horse has learned to easily switch his haunches from outside to inside after much practice of this simple exercise, the rider may progress to Phase 2.

shoulder-in   haunches-in

shoulder-out   haunches-out

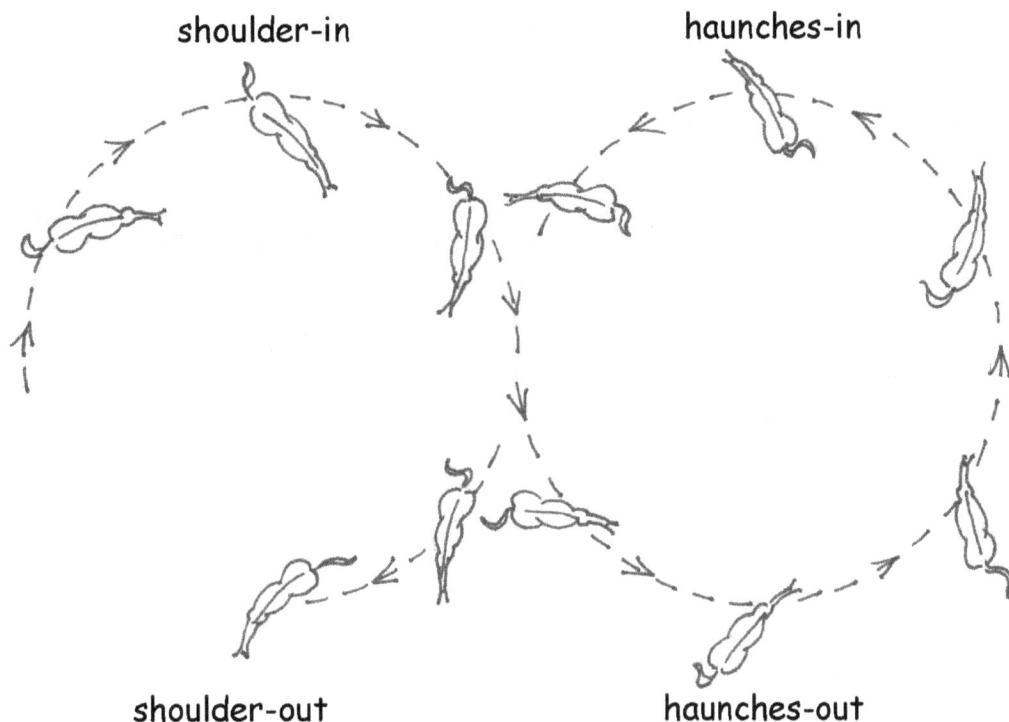

Figure 50 - Shoulder-in; Haunches-out

Phase 2. Beginning the pattern of the same figure eight as in Phase 1, the rider should proceed at the canter while maintaining her horse in the shoulder-in. At the conjunction point between the two circles, the rider should push the horse's haunches outward (haunches-out) and maintain the counter-canter. At the end of the second half-circle, the rider should push the horse's haunches to the inside. If the horse easily changes lead, the rider should canter a few more strides, walk and reward her horse. If the horse does not change leads, the rider should ask the horse one or two more times for a change of lead. Sometimes horses are a little slow to understand what is being demanded. If the horse still does not change leads, the rider should walk and demand a canter departure on the inside lead.

Nota Bene

There are many methods to teach the flying changes but these five methods are classic, simple, and easy to follow. The key to success is to repeat all phases of the exercises preceding the final goal, i.e. the actual flying change.

When the horse understands and is able to perform single changes of lead with ease, the rider should vary the canter's pace to ensure the regularity of the changes and the steadiness of the canter as well as maintaining the horse's impulsion and activity. The changes in pace compels the horse to easily maintain a steady tempo throughout the changes. It is a beneficial exercise to lengthen the canter for three strides and ask for the change of lead. Ask the horse to shorten the canter for three strides and ask for a change of lead.

Nota Bene

Riders should be aware that when a horse truly understands the flying changes, the horse may, for no apparent reason, change leads. This is not a vice but only a phase through which the horse is going. The rider must be compassionate and kind in her response. Horses sometimes tend to act as young children: when they learn a new trick, children and horses may have a tendency to do it all the time, at least for a while.

Troubleshooting

Problem: The horse slows the pace and loses impulsion.

Solution: The rider's inferior aids (seat and legs) should always accompany the horse while her hands maintain a steady but light contact with the horse's mouth. Too much contact with the horse's mouth diminishes the impulsion and thereby impairs the engagement of the horse's posteriors. The rider must always keep the horse active by maintaining the cadence of the gait.

Because the horse does not propel himself any longer and loses the amplification in his strides, the rider's first reaction should be to increase the actions of her legs to round the horse's top line without increasing the pace. Returning to study individual changes and confirming the forward motion while lengthening and shortening the canter strides will correct the problem.

Problem: The horse increases the pace and anticipates the change of lead.

Solution: The rider should regulate the canter by applying one or two half-parades on the opposite side of the existing lead, i.e. left side half-parades on the right lead and vice versa. If the horse ignores the hand action, the rider should revisit the transitions within the canter, i.e. lengthening and shortening the canter.

Problem: The horse is slightly zigzagging during the changes.

Solution: The rider must maintain equal contact on both sides of the horse's mouth. Unequal contact will incite the horse's shoulders to wander left and right. The rider must canter in cadence while maintaining the straightness of the horse's head, neck, and body. The rider must always look where she is going, meaning that the rider should always be focusing on her destination.

Teaching the Tempe Changes of Lead (also known by the swordsmanship expression as the *tact au tact*)

Cantering along the track, the rider should, from time to time, every six or seven strides, ask for a single flying change of lead, making certain that the horse remains in balance, straight and obedient. After each flying change, the rider should begin counting the strides between the changes. Gradually and progressively the rider should change leads at closer intervals by randomly reducing the number of strides between the last change of lead to reduce the horse's anticipation of the lead change. The rider should make certain that her aids are clear and precise and wait for the horse's response without rushing the progression. Resting and rewarding the horse is of key importance.

Practicing the lead changes by varying the number of strides between them will keep the horse alert to the rider's demands. The work requires patience and imagination on the rider's part. A slow and methodical progress should develop the horse's ability to perform many changes of lead in a row. At the Grand Prix level in dressage, fifteen consecutive changes are required, but the horse should be capable of performing more than double this amount.

Maître François Baucher, acclaimed as the father of tempe changes, stipulated that the horse must remain active, in balance, and absolutely straight in his body.

It cannot be emphasized enough that rushing the horse must be avoided. If, at any time, the rider encounters the slightest problem, she should, without hesitation, review the exercises provided in the various methods. When the horse has acquired the skill of changing leads, besides varying the frequency of demanding changes of leads, the rider should vary the pace and vary the patterns being followed. If the horse tries to escape during the changes, it is because the rider does not maintain a comfortable pace for the horse. If the horse changes the pace during the changes, it will be a clear indication that the rider is not in unison with the horse, and that the horse is no longer engaged in the propulsion.

Nota Bene

To allow the horse to be straight, the rider must always maintain equal contact with both reins and maintain a focal point ahead of her.

When the horse is able to change leads consecutively more than ten strides, provided that the study has been prepared properly without force, tempe changes almost become a new gait for the horse. To perform properly, the horse must be happy in this air.

CHAPTER FIVE

The School Trot

The school trot is a slow, cadenced trot. The horse propels his limbs upward by slightly flexing his anterior and posterior joints to cause bending that creates the beginning of elevation and suspension. The horse's trot gains in height what it loses in length. The school trot is similar to a soft, low Passage.

The school trot belongs to the high school movements known in French as *air*. To develop the school trot, the rider should teach the horse to mobilize or activate his posterior limbs by slightly decreasing and increasing a very slow trot. The horse is trotting as slowly as possible but continues in the forward motion without falling into the walk. The horse should learn to promptly change from a slow trot to a slower trot and back to a slow trot without hesitation.

Phase One. Slowing the Trot

Sitting tall in the saddle and resisting with her lower back muscles, the rider should maintain constant contact with lower legs placed somewhat farther back to maintain the activity of the horse's posteriors. The rider's hand should be acting alternately by briefly closing and opening her right hand when the right shoulder is moving backwards and closing and opening her left hand when the left shoulder is retrograding.

To activate the trot, the rider should maintain an erect, but soft upper body. She should act by steadily squeezing both legs simultaneously for two or three strides and give a push with her seat. If necessary, she should apply the whip à propos on the croup if the horse shows signs of laziness. The rider should maintain a light contact with the horse's mouth, without losing contact entirely.

Phase Two. Activating the Walk

At a slow walk, the rider should activate the horse's posteriors by acting with both legs and stimulating the gait by gently tapping on the horse's croup. The whip should be held parallel to the ground and act near the horse's hip angle. The rider should resist with her lower back and hands without pulling on the horse's mouth.

It is important that as soon as the horse shows signs of increased activity, the rider should soften her aids, i.e. a descent of the aids by softening the seat, legs, and hands.

The work-study should be practiced by slowing the trot for a few strides, walking a few strides, and then immediately return to a less slow trot and continue alternating between the trot and walk in this manner. The rider should have the sensation that the horse is dancing.

The rider should alternate the slow and fast speed of the trot to make certain that the horse will maintain the activity of the posteriors and not fall into the walk.

Nota Bene

After the horse has learned the basics of the slow trot, continuing in this mode for too long a period can create monotony and an eventual decrease in activity.

Piaffe and Passage

The Passage is a cadenced trot derived from the trot with a slower tempo than the trot. The horse covers less ground and gains in height what he loses in length. The raised legs mark a slight pause. The horse's forearms should be horizontal to the ground, the canon bone perpendicular to the ground, and the hoof should be level with the middle of the opposite canon bone. The posteriors should be less elevated than the anteriors, with the hoof level with the opposite fetlock. The horse should give the impression of total calm and elegance.

The Piaffe is merely a Passage in place with slightly less marked elevation. The horse should lower his haunches by flexing his loin area. The horse will be highly collected.

The great Masters recommended teaching the Piaffe before the Passage because it is the only gait where certain irregularities of the diagonal bipeds are visible to the naked eye. If the lack of coordination is not corrected, both the Piaffe and most certainly the Passage will lose their natural majestic beauty when each diagonal biped alternately reaches the ground with both hooves perfectly synchronized. If one anterior touches the ground before the posterior, the horse is said to be on the forehand; when the opposite occurs the horse is overloaded behind and loses thrust and his horizontal balance. When one hoof of one diagonal biped reaches the ground before the other, the beauty and the symmetry of the Piaffe and the Passage will be greatly impaired. If the irregularities of the trot are not corrected, once the horse has learned the Passage, it may be too late to correct a lack of symmetry that has been established as habit. If coordination is lacking, the rider should review the transition exercises, various pirouettes, counter-pirouettes and the rein-back tracking to the right and left to correct the problem before continuing any progression in the high level dressage. It cannot be stressed enough that the two hooves of the same diagonal remain synchronized and touch the ground at the same precise time.

The Piaffe

The Piaffe is a very slow cadenced trot progressing forward inch by inch or in place. The horse should mark two equal beats with a flexion of the loins that will increase the engagement of the posteriors without losing impulsion. By lowering his haunches (flexion of the loins) the horse engages, shorten his polygon of sustentation, and as the horse brings his posteriors closer to the anteriors, the distance between the nose and tail will be diminished and will result in collection. Steady cadence in the correct attitude is more important than the elevation of the limbs, the height of which can be low, medium, or high.

The horse can be trained in the Piaffe when the horse is submissive to the rider's aids at the walk and trot and the rider is able to balance the trot between her legs and hands.

Figure 51 - Piaffe

Rider's Aids for the Piaffe (Lateral Aids)

Hands: The hand aids alternate one after the other as follows: The right hand acts lightly with a direct rein of opposition to hold the right anterior leg on the ground and free the horse's left anterior leg, then the left hand acts lightly with a left direct rein of opposition to hold the left anterior on the ground and free the right anterior leg.

Legs: The right leg acts slightly back at the same time with the right hand. The left leg acts slightly back at the same time with the left hand.

Seat: In an imperceptible manner, the rider should alternately increase her weight on the stirrup; for example, increase the weight on the right when the right anterior is grounded (and vice versa for the left).

Teaching the Piaffe

The Piaffe can be taught in five different ways:

1. From the ground;

2. At the halt;

3. By slowing the walk;

4. By slowing the trot; and

5. By slowing the Passage.

Each method of teaching the Piaffe is discussed below.

From the Ground (Work in Hand)

Working the horse in hand has many advantages over the few inconveniences. The advantages are:

i. The horse not having to carry the weight of the rider.

ii. The horse can see the rider at all times.

iii. The rider can see the horse's body. The rider can easily learn to move with the horse.

iv. The rider works with her hands near the horse's mouth and therefore must become sensitive, tactful and precise.

The inconveniences are:

i. The horse possibly being too tall for the rider so that the rider cannot reach over the horse's top line.

ii. The ground may be so deep that the rider cannot easily trot with the horse.

In the following progression, the rider should proceed only to the next phase when the present phase is well-understood by the horse and will obey the rider without hesitation.

99

Figure 52 - Work in hand; the rider walking forward

Phase One.

Tracking left, holding both reins in her right hand under the horse's chin separated by her index finger, with a whip in her left hand, the rider walks parallel to her horse, i.e., the horse's left shoulder is next to the rider's right shoulder (it will be opposite tracking to the right).

Phase Two.

Practice walk—halt—walk transitions many times until the horse becomes accustomed to them. To motivate the horse to move forward, the rider should stimulate the horse by touching the horse with the whip on his left side; to halt the horse, the rider should either use her voice, resist with her hand, or lift the horse's head if the horse does not respond. If the horse is difficult in the downward transitions, the rider should slide two fingers around the noseband and apply a gentle but firm downward check.

Phase Three.

The rider walks backward left shoulder to left shoulder with the horse. The reins are held in the rider's left hand and the whip in her right hand. The rider should hold the whip as if she were holding a tennis racket parallel to the ground. To send the horse forward, the rider should gently apply the whip on the horse's chest; to halt the horse, the rider should either use her voice or slightly lift the horse's head or check. Repeat the exercise on the right side.

Figure 53 - Rider walking backward

Phase Four.

Walking right shoulder to left shoulder with the horse, the rider can teach the horse to trot in hand by progressing in the following separate stages.

Stage 1. The rider trots with the horse at the speed the horse prefers providing that it is not too fast. To obtain the trot, the rider should use a voice command supported by a light tap of the whip on the horse's side. Together, horse and rider will trot for a few strides before the rider asks for a transition to the walk.

After many repetitions, the horse will obey more promptly and eventually slow the trot.

Stage 2. During the trotting phase the rider herself switches to a very forward walk while the horse continues to maintain the trot. After several repetitions, the rider will try to slow the trot until the horse is still trotting, albeit very slowly.

Stage 3. Walking side by side, the rider, without walking faster, demands the trot. After several sessions, the rider should be able to slow the horse's trot by gradually walking even slower.

Stage 4. The rider walks backward left shoulder to left shoulder with the horse. The rider asks the horse to slowly trot forward and give easy transitions to the walk and halt.

Phase Five.

After many transitions of walk—halt—walk—trot—halt—trot—walk—rein-back—walk—trot—rein-back—trot, the rider asks the horse to halt. The rider will lightly tap the horse on the front of his two posterior canon bones to mobilize the horse's hind legs. If the horse shows irregularity in the flexion of one or the other hock joint, the rider should apply the whip to the front of that hind leg at the anterior crease of the joint.

Phase Six.

The rider gradually obtains activity for a slightly longer period and allows the horse to slow the trot to a maximum and to trot in place. To stimulate the horse's hindquarters the rider gently applies the whip on the top of the croup or demands a Gentle Helper to use a long whip on the back of the hind legs.

It is important that the rider never ask too much from the horse at one time and always reward the willingness of the horse by rubbing his eyes gently over closed eyelids (a very sensitive part of the horse's body) and pat him on the neck. The best reward for the horse, however, is to interrupt the work and bring the horse back to his stall.

Mounted

To teach the Piaffe, the horse should not only be able to jump into a trot from a walk, but also from a standstill. After several sessions, the rider should reduce the number of strides at the trot as well as the duration of the halts. These reductions should be made very gradually. The trot should be rather slow, well-defined, but definite. The halts and departs should be rigorously straight.

At the Halt

From a halt the rider demands four steps of rein-back and then immediately mobilizes the horse forward with the whip on the croup. The rider gradually reduces the steps of rein-back to three, two, one, and then none. After repeating this exercise a sufficient number of times, the horse will begin to mobilize himself little by little until he produces steps similar to a Piaffe.

By Slowing the Walk.

Method One.

From a collected walk the rider slows the gait and asks for three or four steps of rein-back. The rider then closes both legs while stimulating the horse on the croup with the whip to mobilize the horse for a few strides. As the horse begins performing something similar to a Piaffe (a few steps of trotting bounces), the rider should gradually reduce the rein-back steps until eliminated.

Method Two.

By seeking to highly activate the horse's hind legs at a very slow walk, the rider will try to decrease the time between the grounding of the anterior and posterior of the same diagonal biped. At the Piaffe, the grounding of the two legs of the same diagonal must be simultaneous. The rider should then shorten the walk to the point of obtaining one walking stride on the spot. After one walking in place stride, the rider sends the horse forward. After several sessions, the rider asks for more walking steps on the spot that will eventually simulate a Piaffe, once the horse is walking in diagonal pairs.

By Slowing the Trot.

The rider practices transitions from walk to trot and from the halt to the trot and vice versa. This work-study brings the horse to a degree of collection that enables him to begin direct preparation for the Piaffe.

The rider balances the horse in a succession of a few strides of trot interrupted by halts; this repeated exercise will gradually shorten the strides as much as possible. The rider should progressively decrease the number of trotting strides and the length of time at the halt. The trot should become as slow as possible while remaining cadenced and energetic.

From a very slow trot, the rider tactfully resists with her lower back with equal soft contact on both reins. To maintain the horse's impulsion, the rider simultaneously holds with both legs to lower the horse's haunches. The rider should feel that the horse's front end is growing, but, in reality, this feeling comes from the lowering of the horse's croup. The whip is tactfully applied on the horse's croup from time to time, tapping in intermittent cadence until the horse bounces from one diagonal biped to the other but still moves forward inch by inch. The horse should not be allowed to travel faster. As soon as the horse has shown activity, the rider should avoid using the whip.

The whip should not be used every stride as the horse may come to rely on the action. Using the whip sporadically will keep the horse alert without becoming reliant on the whip as part of the aiding system.

Study of the Piaffe provides another perfect time to apply the adage:
"Legs without hands and hands without legs."

By Slowing the Passage

Acting with alternate hand actions and resisting with her back, the rider gradually reduces the speed of the Passage to eventually perform the Passage in place. The Piaffe is similar to the Passage in place, but the Piaffe requires less elevation of the limbs and more flexion of the loin area. In both cases, the rider should maintain the cadence of the Piaffe with discreet motion of his/her back. During the transitions, the horse's body must remain absolutely straight.

As soon as the horse produces a semblance of a Piaffe, the rider returns to the walk to avoid anticipation of the rider's aids. The horse should never be allowed to lean on the bit because resting on the rider's hands may permit the horse to disengage his posteriors.

If the rider feels a definite lack of energy as soon as the horse provides a few bouncing steps, the rider should send the horse forward into a medium trot for a few strides and then halt. At a standstill, the rider should drop the reins and allow the horse to completely relax.

Plate 3: Piaffe in front of the Grande Écurie at Versailles. Painting by François Lemaire de Ruffieu.

The rider may also require the assistance of a Gentle Helper who, with a whip applied on the posteriors from the ground, encourages the horse to remain active.

The Piaffe can be low, medium, or high. To obtain more elevation of the limbs, the rider should alternate diagonal aids, i.e. right indirect rein with the left leg slightly back when the horse's right anterior is up and vice versa. The right indirect rein weights the left anterior and frees the right one. The left leg slightly back engages and animates the left posterior. Very discreetly, the rider should burden the stirrup on the side of the posterior that is on the ground.

Troubleshooting

Problem: The horse's feet of one diagonal biped are not properly synchronized.

Solution: The horse's feet in each diagonal biped must be absolutely coordinated with one another and reach the ground simultaneously. If this is not the case, the rider should discontinue the study of the Piaffe and return to the elementary longitudinal exercises with special emphasis on the lateral movements to perfect the pirouette and counter pirouette until synchronization of the horse's hooves has been restored.

Problem: The horse does not lower his haunches by flexing his loins.

Solution: To teach the horse to lower his haunches, the rider should practice the shoulder-in in both directions to lower the horse's haunches one at a time. The rein-back, and the pirouette at the canter also lower the horse's haunches.

Problem: The horse lowers his haunches too much.

Solution: Excessive lowering of the horse's haunches (acculer, meaning to anchor) is a means by which the horse avoids the effort or refuses the work. The rider should simultaneously close both legs in cadence to make certain that the horse stays in the forward mode but does not increase the pace. The rider should not be aggressive but should wait until the horse finds a comfortable slow pace and maintains it. When a very slow cadence and rhythm are correct, the horse should maintain his pace without reducing it.

Problem: The horse is under himself with the front legs instead of alternately lifting them in a vertical plane.

Solution: A horse that is under himself with his front end results from a definite lack of engagement of the posteriors due to poor impulsion. The horse actually sits on his haunches, closes himself and resists with his top line. The rider must stimulate the horse toward the bit with both legs and seat so that he lifts his forehand and is able to move his anteriors forward. The horse will then be able to rebalance himself; his forehand will lift vertically and will give freedom to the anteriors.

Problem: The horse tightens his top line and resists with his back muscles.

Solution: When the rider creates too much tension on the reins, the horse will tighten his back muscles and excessively switch his tail. The rider should maintain light contact in her hands and straighten the horse's shoulders and haunches while maintaining the propulsion so that when the rider reduces the speed, elevation and symmetry is guaranteed.

Problem: The horse becomes lazy.

Solution: The rider should postpone the study and send the horse into a very forward trot while giving him freedom with both hands. If the horse still shows laziness, the rider should make certain that her posture is erect with her heels, hips and shoulders in line with more weight on the stirrups and less weight on the seat.

Problem: The horse becomes heavy on the rider's hands.

Solution: The rider should apply discreet but determinant brief half-halts and ease her leg pressure.

Exercises to Develop the Piaffe

Performing pirouettes at the walk followed by counter pirouettes with activity. The rider should make certain that the horse does NOT cross his legs but flexes his joints so that the horse's legs will gain in height what is lost in crossing.

- Piaffe in a shoulder-in in both directions.
- Transition between the Piaffe to walk to Piaffe.
- Piaffe with the neck and head long and low.
- Piaffe in the half-pass.
- Piaffe pirouette around the haunches and around the shoulders.
- Piaffe pirouette around the horse's center.
- Piaffe between pillars.

Nota Bene

At first, the horse may swish his tail vigorously, but when the Piaffe becomes more natural and comfortable, easier to perform, the tail swishing will gradually diminish until it becomes motionless.

Figure 54 - Four ways to check if the Piaffe is correct

The Passage

The Passage is a very cadenced and elegant air (gait) derived from the trot. The Passage has a clear pronounced time of suspension between the foot falls of the two diagonal bipeds. The horse, in a majestic cadence, gives the impression that he is floating above the ground, hopping from one diagonal pair to the other. The cadence is slower than the regular trot. The horse covers less ground but gains in height what he loses in length. At the Passage, contrary to the Piaffe, the horse does not lower his haunches as much or reduce his sustentation base. The Passage can be low, medium or grand when the elevation is perfect.

At the Passage the horse's legs, which are raised, should mark a slight pause. The forearms are near the horizontal; the canon bones vertical from the ground; and the knees are slightly flexed. The foreleg performs a harmonious and graceful movement. The elevation of the hind legs must be less than the forelegs' for instance, when the toe of the front leg that is elevated should be level with the middle of the opposite canon bone of the grounded front leg. The toe of the hind leg should be level with the fetlock of the opposite grounded hind leg.

Before studying the rudiments of the Passage, the rider should perfect the school trot, reduce the horse's pace, and try to obtain the *doux* Passage (soft Passage or low Passage) with the horse softly bouncing from one diagonal biped to the other without seeking much elevation of the limbs.

When the horse is comfortable with the *doux* Passage the rider should increase the actions of her legs without increasing the pace. At this point the horse will begin to show amplification and elevation of the two distinct diagonal bipeds.

Figure 55 - Passage in front of a mirror

Rider's Aids for the Passage (Diagonal Aids)

The rider's hands, legs, and seat action should be light an imperceptible. The rider should never act with her legs and simultaneously act by pulling with her hands. The maxim,

"Legs without hands; hands without legs"

should be adhered to strictly and meticulously respected. The rider should never try to obtain the Passage by holding the horse back with her reins, but instead, increase the leg action without moving faster.

Hands: The hand acts alternately, one after the other and a little higher.

The right hand softly acts with an indirect rein to free the right anterior and burden the horse's left anterior.

The left hand acts softly with an indirect rein to free the left anterior and burden the right anterior.

Legs: The left leg acts at the same time as the right hand but slightly further back and vice versa for the right leg.

Seat: The rider should discreetly and alternately increases weight on the stirrups, i.e. increase weight on the left when the right anterior is in suspension and vice versa.

Four Methods to Obtain the Passage

Method One: From the Trot.

The rider reduces the cadence or speed of the trot until she feels a cadence similar to the Passage. The rider keeps the horse straight by maintaining equal but light contact with both reins.

The rider increases the action of both legs without allowing the horse to trot faster or slower and maintains the pace by holding the horse with both legs in contact. The horse will find his own balance with his poll being the highest point.

Method Two: From the Piaffe.

The style of the Passage developed from the Piaffe is generally more natural and academic. From the Piaffe, the rider increases the action of her legs and releases the contact with the horse's mouth to allow the horse to move a little more forward. The horse should jump into a Passage.

Method Three: From Counter-changes

When the rider follows the pattern of counter-changes (zigzag in half-pass) at gradually closer intervals, the horse will progressively yield more cadence and elevation. This method should be avoided as it incites the horse to develop a lateral swinging movement that is considered a serious fault.

Method Four. From the Spanish Trot.

The rider reduces the speed from a Spanish trot that can develop into the Passage. This method, however, results in the horse habitually marking an extension of the forelegs that prevents the canon bones from being on the vertical, which is considered to be a fault.

Obtaining More Elevation of the Limbs

Once the horse is comfortable in performing a semblance of the Passage, the rider should work on obtaining more elevation of the limbs so that the horse increases flexion in his leg joints by alternating the application of the diagonal aids.

When the horse's left diagonal pair of legs is on the ground, the rider should act with her right indirect rein of opposition behind the withers along with her left leg slightly behind the girth. When the horse's right diagonal pair of legs is on the ground, the rider should act with her left indirect rein of opposition behind the withers along with a right leg slightly behind the girth. The use of the diagonal aids alternately burdens the legs on the ground and frees the horse's legs off the ground that will allow the horse, with tactful practice, to progressively elevate the limbs.

When the horse becomes more comfortable and is able to elevate his limbs, the rider may be able to produce this elevation by simply alternately increasing the weight on her stirrups, i.e. the rider increases her weight on her left stirrup when the horse's left diagonal pair of legs is on the ground and vice versa when the horse's right diagonal pair of legs is on the ground. When the rider is able to become more discreet in her aids, she will allow the horse to show a more majestic Passage. Remember: the less the rider does, the better.

Nota Bene

The rein contact should be equivalent and soft on both sides of the horse's mouth otherwise all irregularities will become very apparent in the horse's shoulders. If the horse rushes, he will automatically lose the cadence of the Passage. If the rider pulls on the reins, she will reduce and lose the activity.

It is most important to demand many transitions from the grand Passage to the low Passage to develop accuracy and elegance.

Troubleshooting

Problem: The horse swings from one side to the other.

Solution: A horse is incited to swing his body left and right in both the Passage and the Piaffe when the rider does not use her legs simultaneously to maintain the horse's straightness in the propulsion. The swinging motion of the horse is contrary to the beauty of these airs.

Problem: The horse tends to slow the pace of his own initiative.

Solution: The horse should never be allowed to change the pace on his own. When the horse slows the pace on his own, the rider should immediately postpone the exercise that she is practicing and send the horse forward until he comes back in the aids. When the horse anticipates the Passage, he will lose the air by beginning to pull forward and lose activity.

Problem: The horse shows difficulties in flexing his joint and raising his limbs.

Solution: Time and practice will solve this problem. Whenever the rider is introducing a new movement, the rider should proceed with a planned evolution and review all lengthening and lateral exercises and make certain that all aids are properly applied. The horse's flexion can be also improved by work in hand with the help of a Gentle Helper standing slightly behind the horse and gently applying a whip on the crease of the hocks.

Practicing the pirouette and counter pirouette without crossing the limbs at a very slow but active pace will invite the horse to elevate his limbs and better flex his joints.

Problem: The horse loses propulsion.

Solution: A common fault of riders is to push the horse too abruptly to obtain the Passage and at the same time block the forward motion. The horse, of course, slows the pace, loses activity, and loses propulsion.

Exercises to Develop the Passage

- Multiply the transitions between grand Passage, medium Passage and Piaffe.
- On a volte at the Passage, maintain the horse's shoulders and the haunches outside.

- Perform the shoulder-in in the Passage on a straight line and on a circle.
- Perform the half-pass in the Passage.
- Practice the transition from a medium trot to a Passage.
- Practice the transition from a canter to a Passage.
- Perform the Passage while maintaining the horse in a long and low position.

Transition from Piaffe to Passage and from Passage to Piaffe

Theoretically, if both airs are correct and easy to obtain, the transitions should be facile. Nevertheless, if one transition is difficult, it implies that the air in the demanding transition needs more application. For example, in a transition from Passage to Piaffe, if the horse has difficulty switching or maintaining an even tempo, the Piaffe requires more work and vice versa.

During the learning phase of the transitions between Piaffe and Passage, the rider should ask for the transitions as follows: from a high Passage, the rider should ask for a low Passage, to a low Piaffe, to a high Piaffe, or vice versa. With time and practice, the horse should be able to easily change from the high Passage to a high Piaffe or from a low Piaffe to a low Passage.

The transitions from Passage to Piaffe or from Piaffe to Passage require a high degree of collection, submission and obedience.

From the Passage to the Piaffe, the rider must maintain the activity as she reduces the amplification of the stride without changing the cadence until the horse has come back to the Piaffe. The rider must keep both legs closed (resisting) to maintain the impulsion and to prevent the horse from anchoring (acculer) himself or performing a western jog.

From the Piaffe to the Passage, the rider must allow the horse to quietly move forward again as she maintains the same attitude without losing the cadence, amplification and the elasticity of the strides.

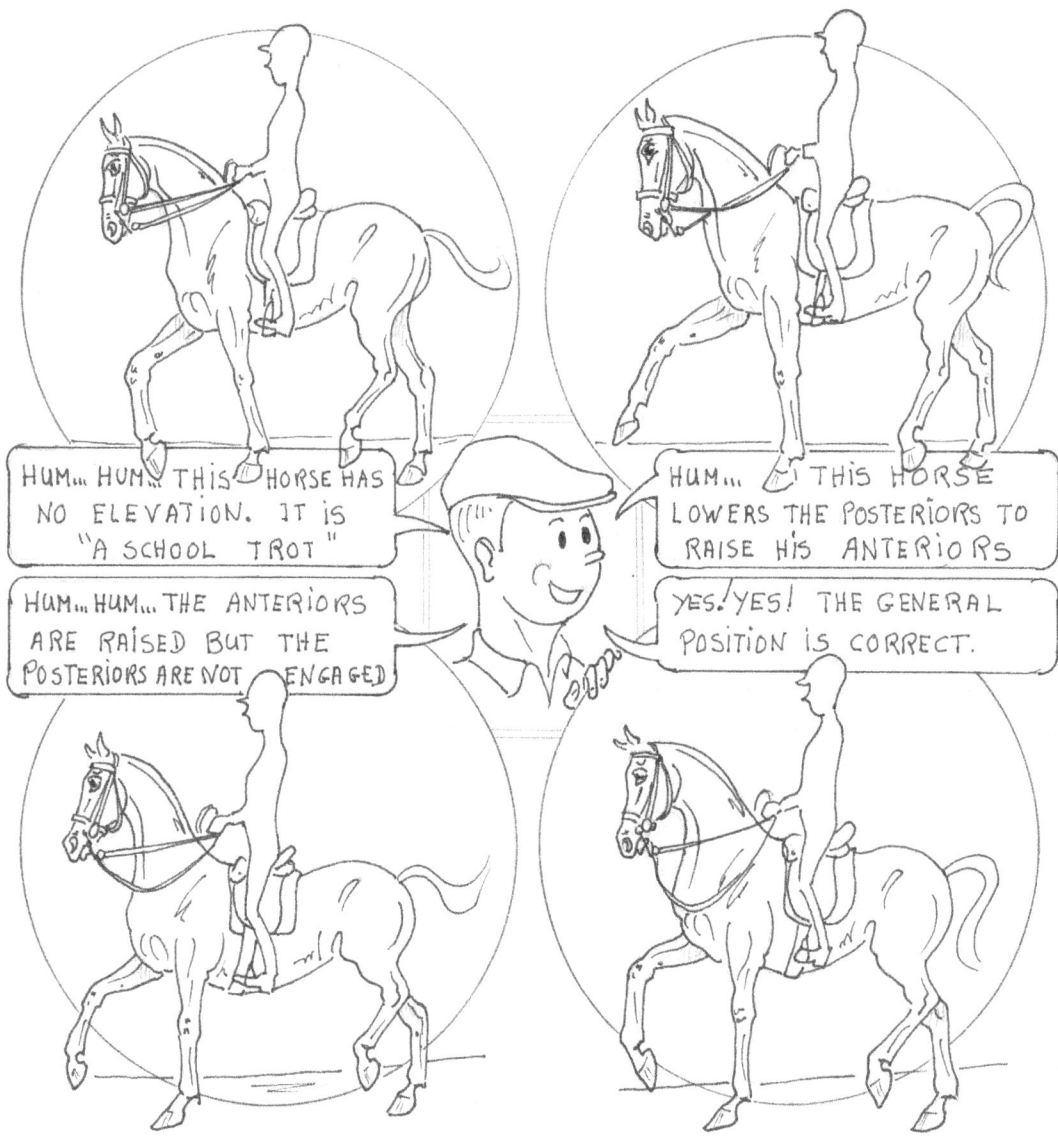

Figure 56 - Showing major faults

EPILOGUE

When the horse is becoming more comfortable at the different gaits and at the various speeds, the rider's natural aids should become silent, i.e. active, but barely perceptible. The horse should learn to remain on automatic pilot (auto-impulsion). The rider's aids become active again if, and only if, or when the horse alters either the speed, equilibrium, or the gait. The horse should be light, meaning that the horse is so well-balanced that the horse can instantly move in any direction at the rider's slightest demand. A horse that propels himself symmetrically becomes comfortable and invites the rider to sit comfortably in the saddle.

Dressage does not end with the high school movements. Dressage opens the door to the airs above the ground, which were introduced in France in the eighteenth century by M. Salmon de La Broue and M. Antoine de Pluvinel de La Baume, who were both students of Giovanni Battista Pignatelli from the Naples Academy in Italy.

M. François Robichon de La Guérinière defined seven airs: the ballotade, the capriole, the courbette, croupade, the mézair, the pesade, and the pas-et-le saut. Today, these airs can mainly be seen in the four major riding academies of Vienna, Saumur, Jerez de la Frontera and Lisbon.

Friendly Tips

- It is most important to always respect and apply the principles of Calm, Forward, and Straight. Position must always precede the action and the aid actions must be disassociated, i.e. legs without hands and hands without legs.

- The rider must take time to educate the horse but not waste time. It is important to repeat the basic exercises often until the horse is able to perform them with ease and suppleness.

- The rider's hand actions should always be preceded by a leg action to better engage the horse's hindquarters.

- The rider should always look in the direction of the motion at eye level.

- The rider should interrupt a work-study with rest periods. When horses are tired, they will not perform to the best of their abilities.

- Always use the same aids to produce the same effects.

- The rider's hands should never cross the crest of the horse's neck. The right hand belongs to the right side and vice versa.

- The rider should always be kind to the horse. A horse that is overpowered is not a horse that is convinced.

- In the evolution of the dressage, the rider should show great patience and softness. Little by little the horse shall acquire all the necessary skills. The rider should proceed from the known to the unknown and from the simplest to the most difficult.

- Horses do not make mistakes, riders do. A movement poorly executed was not explained properly by the rider.

- Always reward the willingness of the horse once he has given what the rider was seeking.

- Never demand more than what the horse can give. Wait until the horse is able.

- A novice dancer cannot become a ballerina in just a few days. The same is true for the horse. It takes time to properly unlock, stretch and supple the horse's muscles. Appropriate repetitions, and daily practice will be required to prevail.

- The rider should always be concerned with impulsion and maintain the horse in front of her legs. The lack of propulsion renders the horse untrainable.

- Always be attentive to the horse's attitude. Riders must know when to change the work-study so that the horse does not become blasé.

- A poor transition should always be redemanded so that the horse does not acquire bad habits.

- To prevent the mistake of pulling on the horse's mouth, the rider should soften her hands and tighten her elbows against her torso.

- For both the horse and rider: A good habit is very difficult to become a conditioned reflex and is easy to lose. A bad habit is very easy to learn and very difficult to lose.

- The rider should always think before acting. The rider should imagine the exercises first, to avoid confusing the horse.

- When a problem occurs, before acting, the rider should pause for a moment and think about the best way to properly handle the situation. If a solution does not come to mind, the rider might ponder, What would she do if she knew the answer? Einstein once said:

"Imagination is more important than genius."

Equestrian Terms and Expressions

Equestrian terms are as exclusive as their definitions and are often derived from the different languages of the countries of their origin. Sometimes these foreign terms have been adopted and often, there is no precise English translation. Riders and trainers must know their meaning. If a term is used that is not understood or clear to a rider, the rider should not hesitate to ask for an explanation. Sometimes, in translation, the English terms have varied the original concept of what the original term was used to describe. Examples include the half-halt and half-parade. The following is a guide of some of the expressions used in *Divide and Conquer Book 1* and *Book 2* and they are often used in equestrian sport.

Equestrian Tact

Equestrian tact is the ability to apply the proper aid at the right time with the right intensity and the right duration.

Halt

The halt (stop) in dressage is to obtain immobility and the horse's calmness in any attitude. It is beneficial in teaching the horse to rebalance himself by engaging both posteriors. When the horse has halted, he must be immobile, straight, and in balance over his four legs. The horse's polygon of sustentation must be square to enable the horse to be ready to move in any direction at the slightest indication of the rider.

The demand of the halt should always be preceded by a discreet resisting action of the rider's legs to engage the horse's posteriors while the actual demand is performed with the rider's center and hand aids used with properly adjusted reins. The horse must learn to promptly and smoothly halt in total balance. The rider should practice the halt very progressively with softness and tact. The halt should first be demanded from a slow walk, then from a working walk, and later from the trot and canter by applying the same tact and subtlety. Correcting a defective halt too soon may allow the horse to develop bad habits and result in the horse contracting his body and refusing to stand immobile. It is best to ignore a poor halt, walk away and demand it again.

Time and practice will solve the problem. The halt, from any gait, should be smooth, soft, and light—similar to a butterfly landing on a flower (as opposed to being abrupt as a ton of bricks falling on the floor).

Half-halt

"The half-halt, as its principal objective, is not to dominate the gait or regulate the speed of the horse, but to transpose the weight of the front end toward the haunches to perfect the horse's balance." — La Guérinière

The half-halt *(demi arrêt)* is a clear but imperceptible rein action executed by the rider's hand(s). The goal is to eliminate a resistance of weight due to the horse being on his forehand. By reestablishing the poll at its proper level in rapport with the neck, the horse will be able to carry himself in his natural attitude. The half-halt has no effect on either the gait or the pace.

The half-halt is a clear but discreet upward action executed by the rider with one or two hands that is immediately followed by a "descent of the hands" (yielding). The rider should lift one or two hands vertically, with her fingernails facing up while holding the reins tightly. The action should give the rider the impression of lifting a heavy weight. The rider, by raising the horse's neck and head, will allow the horse to transfer the excess weight from the forehand to the hindquarters so that the horse is more able to rebalance himself. The rider should always remember that the leg actions (squeezing of the legs) must precede the hand action.

To perform a half-halt, the rider acts as follows:

1. The rider is properly positioned on the saddle with both legs maintained in steady contact and closed around the horse's sides. Both reins are equally adjusted.

2. The rider closes both hands and rotates her wrists (supinates).

3. The rider swiftly elevates her hand(s) in a vertical plane without pulling or loosening the contact with the horse's mouth.

4. The rider immediately lowers and yields with relaxed fingers.

5. Immediately following the half-halt, the rider reestablishes a light contact with the horse's mouth so that the horse stays in balance.

The term half-halt *(demi arrêt)* is misleading in that two words half and halt have no association with the actual action of the half-halt and the halt. At the dawn of the revolution in 1789, French noblemen fled the country and took with them their equestrian knowledge. French riding terms could not always be literally translated, and as a result, some of the nuances implied in the French term were lost or misinterpreted.

The French riding term, *demi arrêt*, has been translated as the half-halt giving the impression that it is somewhat of a halt or slowing of the pace, but in reality, the horse only transfers his weight from front to back and has neither an effect on the gait nor the speed.

Half-parade

A half-parade *(demi parade)* is a brief lateral action in which the rider uses the direct rein of opposition when the horse is resisting or is not responding to a demand of transition. The action should be made within the time of one stride. The half-parade is the rider's action to reorganize the horse's pace by regulating his forehand without losing the engagement of his posteriors; the horse must be obedient and balance himself within the forward motion. The horse must not stop, but must immediately regulate his pace by transferring his body weight from front to back.

To perform a half-parade, the rider acts as follows:

1. The rider stimulates the horse's forward motion with both legs without increasing the speed.

2. Within the time of one stride, the rider, while resisting with her lower back, acts several times in succession using a direct rein of opposition without pulling on the rein.

3. The rider immediately yields with both hands as soon as she feels the horse has slowed the pace and becomes obedient again.

4. The rider immediately reestablishes a light contact with the horse's mouth. Although the terms half-parade and half-halt are frequently interchanged, each is used in different instances. The term, half-parade, is used when the rider is trying to regulate the horse's body weight evenly between his forehand and the horse's engaged posteriors. The term, half-halt is used when the horse resists because the horse has lack of balance.

Combined Effect

The combined effect *(effet d'ensemble)* is a powerful but kind means of domination that a rider may use to reach the higher levels in dressage. While it is an effective means to calm the horse, it also has a dominating effect which can, used improperly, cause the horse to become cold to the rider's legs. It is not an aid that should be used by an inexperienced rider. The combined effect has an action over the horse's entire body to render the horse to the rider's disposal. The combined effect involves simultaneous hand and leg actions and is an exception to the maxim:

"Legs without hands and hands without legs."

The combined effect is first taught when the horse is standing still and immobile as follows:

1. While the horse is motionless, the rider gradually tightens all fingers on both equally adjusted reins.

2. The rider then tightens both legs placed a little further forward than usual to avoid confusing the horse and impairing the response to the forward motion.

3. The rider's legs gradually become tighter beginning in the rider's calves and gradually acting lower in the leg around the spur level.

4. At the slightest yielding of the horse's jaws (cession of the mouth) the rider releases her aids (descent of the aids).

The result of the combined effect is expressed by the beginning of collection; all of the horse's contractions are ceasing in his mouth as well as at the poll. The horse becomes light and obedient.

If the horse fails to understand initially and remains inert, the rider should slightly vibrate (the violinist's tremolo) her fingers on one or two reins without increasing the leg action. The rider should wait until the horse clearly responds, becomes relaxed and has understood the action of the combined effect. If needed, the rider may apply the same demands progressively at the walk, trot, and finally at the canter.

Long and Low (extension d'encoloure)

The horse is said to be long and low when the horse travels with his neck low and his nose ahead of the vertical and near the ground. Benefits of the long and low attitude include:

- stretching and building the horse's top line (ilio spinal muscles, ligaments and tendons)
- shortening and reinforcing his abdominal grid
- improving the engagement of this posteriors
- developing his balance

At the beginning, the long and low attitude has the inconveniences of distinctly increasing the weight on the horse's forehand and inciting the horse to increase his speed. Because more weight is on the horse's forehand, the horse may begin to stumble on one or two front legs.

The initial rushing period as the horse learns to have his posteriors catch up with his anteriors. The horse will regain and improve his natural balance and will no longer rush or stumble. Sometimes it is preferable to tolerate a temporary inconvenience to achieve the desired results.

Nota Bene

When the horse is confirmed in the upper level, asking the horse to travel long and low will improve engagement and balance. This position can be applied to all exercises, i.e. the shoulder-in, haunches-in, half-pass, Piaffe, Passage, and canter etc.

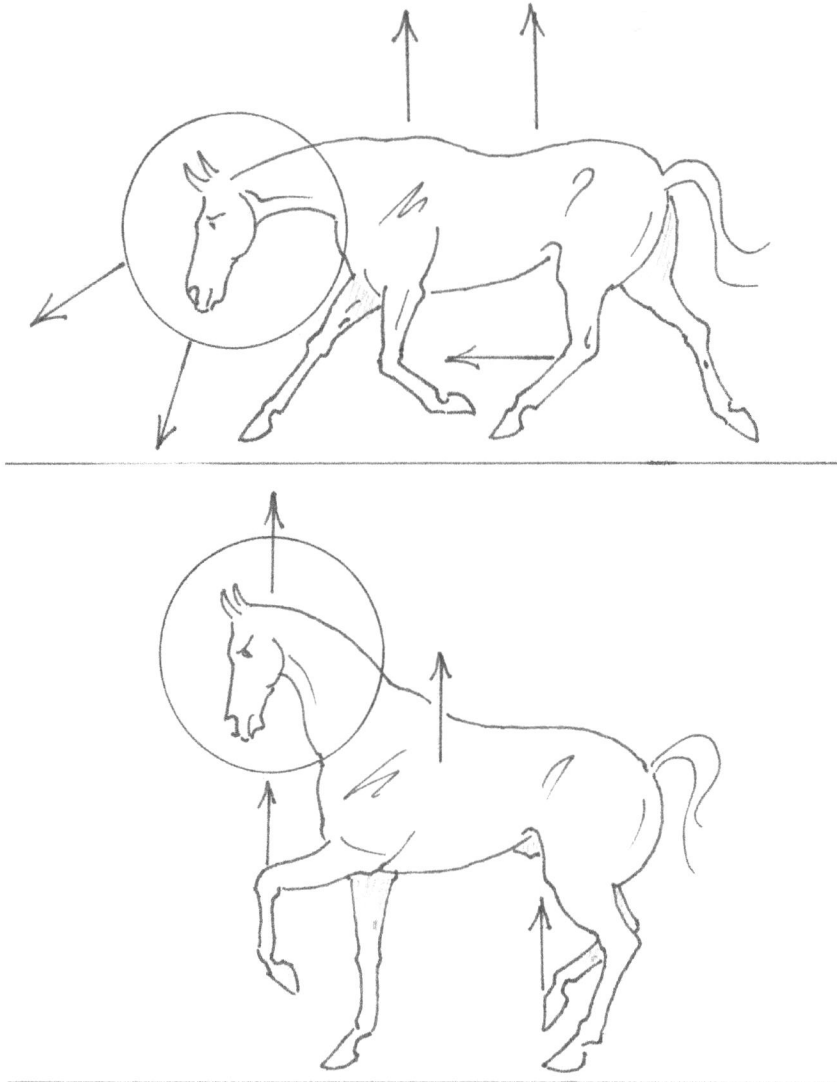

Figure 57 - Low and high

Nota Bene

A horse can also work in a long and round position. The horse will be in a low frame with his head behind the vertical. In only a few cases, this exercise might be acceptable providing that the stretching time is of short duration. Scientific studies indicate that such a position should not be held for more than one minute or so because it may harm the horse to the extent of causing permanent physical damage.

Deep and Low

In this attitude, the horse's neck is curled so that his nose reaches his chest. The position is neither physically nor psychologically advantageous to the horse and may cause harm. It is a despotic means of domination. In this posture, the horse can neither retaliate nor respond.

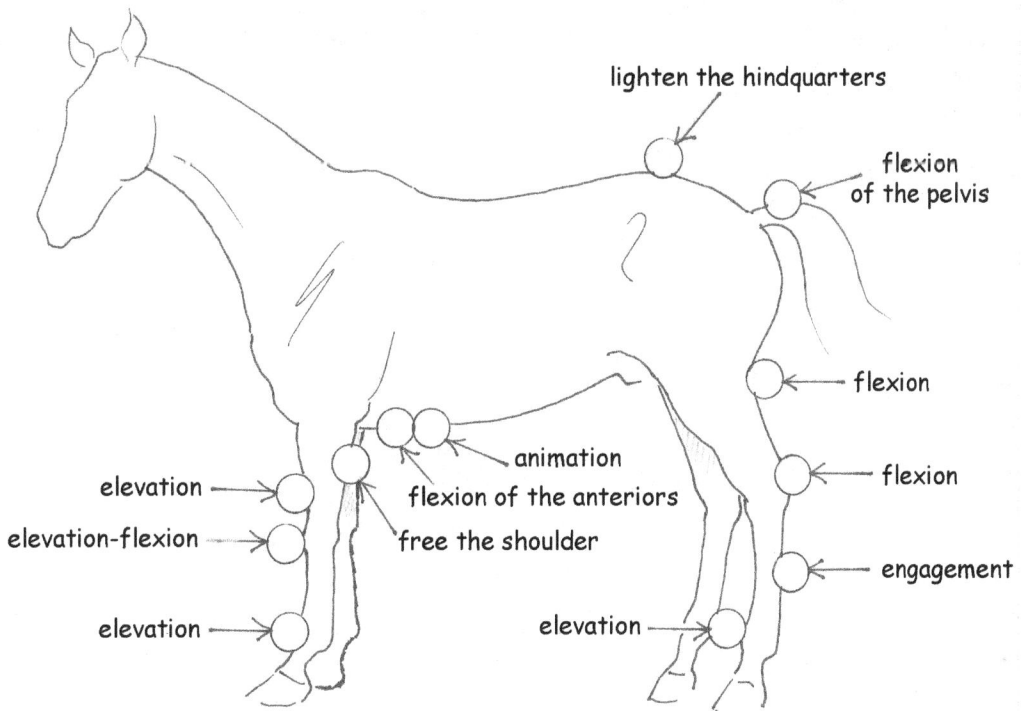

Figure 58 - Reactions to whip

History of the Third Rein

The third rein action is a remnant from antiquity that has nearly disappeared in modern riding. The third rein was associated with Persian riders and known as Akma. The Persian Akma is the ancestor of the French cavesson, the Spanish bosal and the American hackamore.

Persian horsemen circa 550 B.C. (and perhaps even in earlier civilizations of people from the Steppes) out of necessity concluded that for better use, horses had to be well-balanced, straight, should flex their loins, engage their posteriors, raise the base of their neck and flex at the poll. All of these characteristics are prerequisites for collection.

In addition to the regular bridle with one pair of reins, a third rein was hooked or looped to be embedded in the noseband over the center of the horse's nasal bone. In this position the third rein was at the correct angle that, when tweaked, would induce the horse to flex at the poll (atlas-axis). The tweaking was produced from the side; it was not a pulling action from front to back because the desired flexion is not an up and down nodding gesture but a slight side slipping of the horse's head, which, today, is referred to as lateral flexion.

The third rein or *akma* was used into the nineteenth century until it was replaced with the use of a double bridle.

Figure 59 - May the horse be with you

XENOPHON PRESS LIBRARY

www.XenophonPress.com

Xenophon Press is dedicated to the preservation of classical equestrian literature. We bring both new and old works to English-speaking riders.

30 Years with Master Nuno Oliveira, Henriquet 2011

A New Method to Dress Horses, Cavendish 2017

A Rider's Survival from Tyranny, de Kunffy 2012

Another Horsemanship, Racinet 1994

Austrian Art of Riding, Poscharnigg 2015

Breaking and Riding: Principles of Dressage and Equitation, Fillis 2017

Classic Show Jumping: the de Nemethy Method, de Nemethy 2016

Divide and Conquer Book 1, Lemaire de Ruffieu 2016

Divide and Conquer Book 2, Lemaire de Ruffieu 2017

Dressage in the French Tradition, Diogo de Bragança 2011

Dressage Principles Illuminated, Expanded Edition, de Kunffy 2017

École de Cavalerie Part II, Robichon de la Guérinière 1992, 2015

Equine Osteopathy: What the Horses Have Told Me, Giniaux 2014

François Baucher: The Man and His Method, Baucher/Nelson 2013

Great Horsewomen of the 19th Century in the Circus, Nelson 2015

Gymnastic Exercises for Horses Volume II, Eleanor Russell 2013

H. Dv. 12 Cavalry Manual of Horsemanship, Reinhold 2014

Handbook of Jumping Essentials, Lemaire de Ruffieu 2015

Handbook of Riding Essentials, Lemaire de Ruffieu 2015

Healing Hands, Giniaux, DVM 1998

Horse Training: *Outdoors and High School*, Beudant 2014

Learning to Ride, Santini 2016

Legacy of Master Nuno Oliveira, Millham 2013

Lessons in Lightness, Mark Russell 2016

Methodical Dressage of the Riding Horse, Faverot de Kerbrech 2010

Racinet Explains Baucher, Racinet 1997

Science and Art of Riding in Lightness, Stodulka 2015

The Art of Riding a Horse or Description of Modern Manege in Its Perfection, D'Eisenberg 2015

The Art of Traditional Dressage, Volume I DVD, de Kunffy 2013

The Ethics and Passions of Dressage Expanded Ed., de Kunffy 2013
The Forward Impulse, Santini 2016
The Gymnasium of the Horse, Steinbrecht 2011
The Horses, a novel, Elaine Walker 2015
The Italian Tradition of Equestrian Art, Tomassini 2014
The Maneige Royal, de Pluvinel 2010, 2015
The Portuguese School of Equestrian Art, de Oliveira/da Costa 2012
The Spanish Riding School & Piaffe and Passage, Decarpentry 2013
To Amaze the People with Pleasure and Delight, Walker 2015
Total Horsemanship, Racinet 1999
Training with Master Nuno Oliveira double DVD set, Eleanor Russell 2016
Truth in the Teaching of Master Nuno Oliveira, Eleanor Russell 2015
Wisdom of Master Nuno Oliveira, de Coux 2012

Available at www.XenophonPress.com

www.ingramcontent.com/pod-product-compliance
Lightning Source LLC
Chambersburg PA
CBHW061955090426
42811CB00006B/947